MY WWII DIARY

AND THE

WAR EFFORT

WITH WAR NEWS DAY BY DAY

ALSO BY THE AUTHOR

Ballads of the North and South
Civil War Stories
Battle of Trevilian Station
Clash of Sabres—Blue and Gray
The War and Louisa County, 1861-1865
Train Running for the Confederacy, 1861-1865
AN EYEWITNESS MEMOIR
Confederate War Stories, 1861-1865
Eyewitness to War, 1861-1865
Courier for Lee and Jackson
and
THE AWARD WINNING
Confederate Letters and Diaries, 1861-1865

ABOUT THE AUTHOR

The author has had a long and distinguished career in the United States Air Force where he received numerous awards for outstanding and meritorious service. At one time he was a member of a Task Force in the Office of the Personnel Advisor to the President, The White House. He was a member of the War Department Personnel Research Council and was assigned to key executive positions in three major Air Force components that contributed significantly to the direct war-time support of aircraft procurement, industrial production and combat readiness.

He was a member of the Federal Personnel Councils of Cincinnati, Chicago, San Francisco, and Anchorage, Alaska.

He has written or edited ten previous books about the War Between the States, including his award-winning "Confederate Letters and Diaries, 1861-1865."

He has a master's degree in American Military History and holds membership in the Bonnie Blue Society which is based on his scholarly research and published literature. He is a member of the Society of Civil War Historians, the Military Order of the Stars and Bars, Sons of the American Revolution, the Ohio State University Alumni Association and four Virginia Historical Societies.

MY WWII DIARY

AND THE

WAR EFFORT

WITH WAR NEWS DAY BY DAY

Walbrook D. Swank
Colonel, USAF, Ret.

 Burd Street Press

Walbrook D. Swank, Colonel, USAF, Ret.
4327 Frederick's Hall Road
Mineral, VA 23117

This Burd Street Press book
was printed by
Beidel Printing House, Inc.
63 West Burd Street
Shippensburg, PA 17257 USA

In respect for the scholarship contained herein, the acid-free paper used in this book meets the guidelines for permanence and durability of the Committee on Production Guidelines for Book Longevity of the Council on Library Resources.

For a complete list of available publications
please write
Burd Street Press
Division of White Mane Publishing Company, Inc.
P.O. Box 152
Shippensburg, PA 17257 USA

Cover Art: "Old Crow P-51D Mustang" by Raymond A. Waddey, from The Hamilton Collection.

Fighter Ace C. E. "Bud" Anderson was the pilot of "Old Crow."
Cloud cover was thick as the P-51D Mustang escorted the B-17 bombers into enemy territory. The pilot could barely see the ground below. Unexpectedly, the clouds began to thin, revealing the enemy countryside . . . an omen that the day's mission would be a success.

Library of Congress Cataloging-in-Publication Data

Swank, Walbrook D. (Walbrook Davis)
    My WWII diary and the war effort with war news day by day / Walbrook D. Swank.
        p.   cm.
    Includes bibliographical references and index.
    ISBN 1-57249-023-3 (alk. paper)
    1. Swank, Walbrook D. (Walbrook Davis)--Diaries. 2. World War, 1939-1945--Personal narratives, American. 3. United States. Army--Biography. 4. Soldiers--United States--Diaries. I. Title.
D811.5.S926 1996
940.54'4973--dc20   96-35261
    [B]   CIP

TO AMERICA'S HOME FRONT WARRIORS
WHO FUELED THE ARSENAL OF DEMOCRACY
IN WORLD WAR II

CONTENTS

ILLUSTRATIONS

PREFACE

This is the story of the contribution of one member of the Army Air Forces to the war-time challenge of meeting the manpower requirements of the nation in the research, engineering, development, procurement, production and inspection of military aircraft and equipment to assure victory through air power.

The Air War Plan submitted to the president a few months before Pearl Harbor, among other things, called for the creation of an air force of more than 2,000,000 men and upwards of 88,000 planes. A few days after Pearl Harbor the Air Force recommended the manning level be increased to 2,900,000 men and officers.

President Roosevelt's initial call for 50,000 airplanes in 1940 soon boosted to 125,000, called for ingenuity and Herculean efforts by American industry to attain production goals.

"American war production now exceeds that of Germany," said Brigadier General Arthur W. Vanaman, Commanding General, Army Air Corps Materiel Center, Wright Field, Ohio, to a Jefferson Day dinner meeting in Akron, Ohio, on 13 April 1942. "But," he continued, "it is relatively small compared with the vast totals that will be required."

The general had returned six months earlier from Germany, where he had been assistant military attaché for air. During the eighteen months prior to his address, the Army Air Corps had let contracts totaling $16,000,000,000, three times as much business as the entire automobile industry in its best year, he said.

"We are generally conceded to be superiors in the field of heavy four-engine bombers, but the Germans recently have developed new types which may challenge the American B-24, or flying fortresses," Vanaman said.

"We, however, are doing some development work on our own hook."

Praising American pursuit craft, the general said, "Two pursuit planes, The Republic P-47 and the Lockheed P-38, are the only airplanes in the world today that are making an honest 400 miles per hour with a full military load."

General Vanaman became a Nazi prisoner of war after his plane was shot down over German territory in June 1944. He is believed to be the only American general to parachute behind the German lines.

The author was a member of the general's staff and served as assistant administrative executive.

Though perhaps less exciting and glamorous than the warriors on the war's battle fronts, those who served in essential home front activities were no less vital cogs in making the flywheel of the arsenal of democracy the key to total allied victory.

ACKNOWLEDGMENTS

I am indebted, and express my deep appreciation, to these contributors, and others, who made the work possible:

Patricia L. Jennings, Associate Project Manager, Product Development, The Hamilton Collection, Jacksonville, Fla., for permission to use the art on the book cover.

Colonel Thomas Scanlon of the USAF Aid Society, Washington, D.C., and Lou Reda of Lou Reda Productions, Inc., Easton, Pa., for permission to use portions of material from the 1944 issue of the Official Guide to the Army Air Forces.

Mark W. Ridley, Library Specialist, Center for Air Force History, Bolling AFB, D.C., for biographical information.

John D. Weber, Command Historian, HQ, Air Force Materiel Command, W-PAFC, Ohio, for unit designation information.

INTRODUCTION

At the close of the first decade of the twentieth century I was fortunate to have been born in the United States and in the beautiful Shenandoah Valley of Virginia—the Old Dominion. Incredible events have occurred in the country and the world since 1910. When I began this diary I must have had a philosophical, apprehensive and ominous view of things to come.

In 1938, at the age of twenty-seven, in Columbus, Ohio, I began to keep a brief daily diary of major events, business and personal thoughts and observations about life and world events. I prefaced the first of my eleven five-year diaries with these words: "This diary is begun because I feel that the next five years will see great changes in world affairs and in my life. Love, sorrow, pathos, anxiety, worry, sickness, fun, war, happiness—life itself—ever changing, ever turbulent."

How perceptive this observation turned out to be! These were stressful times. Prayers lightened the burden and gave us strength. Tolerance, sustained effort, a sense of humor, flexibility and patience were essential to successfully cope with the pressures of the workplace.

ABBREVIATIONS

AACMD — Army Air Corps Materiel Division 10/25/26
AAF — Army Air Force
AAFATSC — Army Air Force Air Technical Service Command 8/31/43
AAFMC — Army Air Force Materiel Command 3/9/42
AAFMC — Army Air Force Materiel Center
AAFMD — Army Air Force Materiel Division
AC — Air Corps
AD — Active Duty
AGO — Adjutant General's Office
AMC — Air Materiel Command
ASC — Air Service Command
CAPD — Central Air Procurement District
CBI — China, Burma, India Theater of War
CCC — Civilian Conservation Corps
CG — Commanding General
CIO — Congress of Industrial Organizations
CPO — Civilian Personnel Officer
EPD — Eastern Procurement District
FDR — President Franklin D. Roosevelt
GI's — Enlisted Men in the Armed Forces
GMC — General Motors Corporation
HQ — Headquarters
LA — Los Angeles
MC — Materiel Command
MCPD — AAF Midcentral Procurement District
NYC — New York City
OCAC — Office, Chief of Air Corps
ONG — Ohio National Guard
OPM — Office of Production Management
ORC — Officers Reserve Corps
POE — Port of Embarkation

QM	—Quartermaster
QM-Res.	—Quartermaster Reserve Corps
RAF	—Royal Air Force
SF	—San Francisco
UMW	—United Mine Workers
UN	—United Nations
US	—United States
USAF	—United States Air Force
USCS	—United States Civil Service
WF	—Wright Field
WPA	—Works Projects Administration
W-PAFB	—Wright-Patterson Air Force Base

CHAPTER I

PRE-PEARL HARBOR

The following is a brief chronological diary of major concerns and happenings through these turbulent years—over 3,000 days. Only significant daily entries are recorded, and they begin in January 1938 when Adolf Hitler's Nazi troops were invading countries in Europe.
Comments about the daily entries are in brackets. [   ]

1938

Jan. 15　Went with two friends to Circleville, Ohio, to see fortune teller. My future—"Will marry my girl [Jane Orr] July-August 1938. My parents will move from Florida. Promotion seen. Death, war, uncertain 1941. Will marry again later in life. Inheritance seen."

[Except for the date of predicted marriage the prophesy was completely correct.]

Feb. 10　Sure would like to have a home of my own to go to at night. Tired of bachelorhood.

March 1　Paid my income taxes today. $1.89.

12　Hitler's troops marched in Austria.

17　Met Janie [my fiancee] three years ago today [1935].
Working on my Officers' Reserve Corps courses.

April 3　First date with Janie—Three years ago today [1935].

20　Streetcar strike in Columbus, Ohio. People ride in ambulances, on skates and bikes.

— 1 —

June 8   Went to top of AIU Building. Tallest in Columbus, Ohio.

10   Bought used 1936 Oldsmobile Coupe for $527.00. Got $271.71 for my '35 Plymouth.

11   Bought my first straw hat.

13   Janie's 22nd birthday.

22   Joe Louis knocked out Max Schmeling in first round. *[Louis was the world heavyweight boxing champion. Schmeling was from Germany.]*

27   Received Harrisonburg, Va. newspaper from Dad with article about his brother who was elected mayor.

July 8   Janie's sister had her first child, Cynthia. Born 2 A.M.

21   Cynthia's mother fainted.

28   Cynthia's mother has a clot in her leg.

31   My best friend, Norman Tharp, and I leave 4:30 A.M. in rain for Washington, D.C. Arrive 4 P.M.

Aug. 1   Norman woke me in our tent at Washington Tourist Camp at 7 A.M. Went to Mt. Vernon and Arlington National Cemetery.

2   Left for New York City. Arrived 5 P.M. Hotel Chesterfield.

3   Breakfast at automat. Took 40 mile boat ride around Manhattan island. Saw Paul Whiteman at CBS. Shook hands and talked with Jack Dempsey and had a drink at his restaurant. *[Jack Dempsey was the former world heavyweight boxing champion.]*

4   Took in Broadway, Times Square, 5th Avenue, Macy's. "Wrong Way" Corrigan arrived on steamer *Manhattan* and the town went wild. *[Corrigan was to make a trans-western flight but in error landed in Ireland.]*

5   Norman and I left 3:45 A.M. for Columbus. Arr. 9:30 P.M. Total 1,288 mile trip.

8   Lee Shield passed the Ohio State Bar exam. *[Lee Shield was my brother-in-law.]*

27   Jane and I went downtown to shop and then to get a couple hamburgers. I had only 26¢ and the bill was 31¢. Oh me, they let us eat but I owe 5¢!

Sept. 8   Appeared before Officers' Reserve Board of Officers to determine if I qualify for appointment in the Officers' Reserve Corps.

13   Hitler demands autonomy for German minority in Czechoslovakia. It looks like war with Mussolini on his side if he does not get it.

14   Looks like war in Europe. Germany and Italy vs. England, France and Russia over Czechoslovakian Sudeten area.

16   Hitler demands Sudeten area be granted annexation by Plebiscite. Czechs will not grant this as England asks.

23   Hitler and Chamberlain's discussions collapse. France, England, Russia and Czechoslovakia mobilizing. Europe aflame.

27   96 hours will see the world at war or peace. Chamberlain talks on radio.

29   Hitler holds conference in Munich with Mussolini, Chamberlain and Daladir.

Oct. 7   Janie and I got 5 hamburgers for 10¢ at Keome Dome.

8   Took oath of office as 2d Lt. QM. Res. Request active duty.

15   Janie and I attend formal dance at Officers' Club, Ft. Hayes.

17   Got measured for my uniform.

18   Received letter of congratulations from Major General Henry Giffins, the quartermaster general, also orders for active duty tour beginning 20 November, my birthday!

Nov. 7   Got my uniform today.

21   Reported for active duty, assigned to Post QM, Ft. Hayes.

Dec. 24   Played 18 holes of golf with my father-in-law, Ralph Orr.

25   Received 22 lovely gifts. 9 from Janie. Xmas at Orr's.

31   Have a quart of 7-Crown and 1 pint of 5-Crown Seagrams left from Christmas. Expect to take care of the pint at Bernice's tonite.

1939

Jan. 7	Income tax papers received today. Oh me!
21	To Officers' Club Dance at the Neil House Hotel.
28	Ran out of gas en route to work. On the way home broke axle and wheel came off!
Feb. 3	Snow and ice—more worry. Collided with another car at N. Grant and 2nd Ave. Damaged fenders and wheels.
8	Dad and Mom at Orlando, Fla. Sold 60 boxes of oranges at .40 a box.
10	A taxicab dented my fender tonite.
22	Had brakes relined today.
March 3	Major Bessie is apparently applying some of the suggestions I made to him regarding the Motor Repair Shop.
15	Hitler takes Czechoslovakia.
19	Hitler wants Rumania.
21	Serious damage to my car in accident. Driver taken to police station. $143.04 damage estimate.
30	2nd Lt. Lloyd Le May, QM-Res. visited me to find out about provisions in the Defense Bill for Reserve Officers. *[Lieutenant Le May is the brother of General Curtis Le May, famous commander of bomber commands.]*
April 4	All recommendations made in my January letter to Major Bessie are being carried out but one. *[Major Bessie was the asst. quartermaster, HQ 5th Corps Area, Ft. Hayes, Ohio.]*
6	Italy about to take Albania.
7	Mussolini invades Albania.
12	Applied for active duty with the Army in Panama.
20	Mr. Lewis told me of Major Bessie's great pleasure with my report on Operations of the Motor Repair Shop.
May 19	Nazi within 70 miles of Paris.
20	Nazi troops heading toward French Channel ports. National Defense Bill being hurried in Congress.

June 8   King George VI and Queen Elizabeth arrive in Washington.

12   Received a stinging letter from Mom giving me the devil for thinking about getting married. That's the last straw. I've heard it for 28 years.

27   Wrote letter to Mom and Dad telling them of my stand.

July 1   To Ft. Knox, Ky. for two week active duty tour.

3   I was made asst. adjutant to the quartermaster. In charge of fire drill squads.

5   Made platoon commander. Lecture and Drill.

6   Lecture and drills A.M. Gas drill. Attacked field target P.M.

7   Took to the field on exercise in 6 trucks. 160 miles. Saw Lincoln's birthplace in Kentucky.

11   Trip to Jeffersonville Quartermaster Depot.

13   Observed infantry and artillery attack and chemical warfare service mortar firing. Visited QM installations at Ft. Knox.

31   I bought Janie a wedding ring.

Aug. 5   Won a golf ball for getting in a 15 foot circle in the *Columbus Citizen* Newspaper Ring Contest.

23   Nazi-Soviet Pact signed. Looks bad for England, France and Europe in general.

25   Hitler demands "Free Hand" in Eastern Europe. Tense conditions.

31   Britain and France backing Poland in war of nerves.

Sept. 1   Germany invades Poland. England and France tell Hitler to withdraw or they will fight.

2   Jane and I were married at 4:30 P.M. Saturday by Reverend Gordon, Glen Echo U.P. Church. Reception at Jane's home. Left for Lake Erie. Stayed at Hotel Antler's Lorain, Ohio. War in Europe. President Roosevelt talks to the nation.

15   Dad and Mom sell their home in Florida.

Sept. 16	Charles Lindbergh spoke on radio advising US to stay out of European war.
17	Russians march into Poland.
21	President Roosevelt addresses Congress on the war.
28	Warsaw falls to the Nazi.
Oct. 6	Hitler tells Reichstag he wants peace in Europe. England and France turn him down.
15	Mom and Dad arrive in Harrisonburg, Va.
17	Nazi planes attack English naval bases.
21	Looks like mobilization is not far off.
22	Drove 377 miles to Harrisonburg to see Mom and Dad at Helbert Hotel.
26	Took Skyline Drive to the Capitol in Washington and visited Ft. Meade where we used to live.
Nov. 2	This is one of the first nights Janie and I have spent the evening at home. Wish it was an everyday occurrence. We spend too much time at her home.
4	President Roosevelt signs repeal of the Arms Embargo Law.
20	My 29th birthday. The last of the 20's. Oh me! I'm aging! Received a card from Janie with 2¢ postage due.
30	Applied for transfer to Air Corps Reserve. Don't expect to make it but will give it a try. Russia attacks Finland.
Dec. 7	Spent the entire evening at home. Thank goodness.
9	Janie and I shopped. Then to her home till 11 P.M. Oh, I wish we could spend some time where we pay rent.
11-13-14	Letters from Mom and Dad talking about the other. Oh me!
14	Stayed home tonite—thank goodness.
18	Getting ready for Christmas but broke!
19	Wonder what the new year will bring.
31	The last day of a terrific decade and year.

1940

Jan.   A new decade. A new year. What is in store for me and this cockeyed world? Only time will tell. I hope for the best. Expect many changes—destiny.

10   Radiogram from HQ USAAF to ORC 5th Corps Area stated they had enough Reserve officers on duty in the Air Corps. So guess my hopes for active duty are off until a catastrophe happens. Attended ONG drill.

11   Had another auto accident this A.M. en route to work. A woman skidded sideways on snow and ice and stopped and I hit her.

12   Up to Janie's home again tonite till 10 P.M. right from work. Home life isn't what I once expected it to be.

13   To Janie's home again tonite as usual till 11:10 P.M.

16   In the dog house for having had a beer or two.

21   From noon on up to Janie's home. Would be great to have a home of one's own.

22   I had hoped to stay home tonite with my wife but she had to take laundry to her home again. I stayed home and washed dishes, mopped and made the bed.

23   Hoo Rah! At home tonite!

25   Boy, it's sure good to spend an evening at home. Nothing like it.

27   Up to Janie's home again tonite 9:30-12:30 P.M.

28   I weigh 164 lbs. Gained 20 lbs. since I got married.

29   Finns defeating the Russian invaders.

30   Janie went to her home to cook dinner for all but her mother and dad then went out to dinner.

31   Pay day and all is gone, Janie at her mother's—it's her birthday.

Feb. 4   At Janie's home till 11 P.M. again.

6   Received 605 lbs. of household goods from my parents. They left for Florida.

8   Stayed home tonite. Hot dog!

Feb. 9   We went to see "Gone With the Wind." $1.13 per person. The dear old South. To Janie's home for dinner as usual.

13   I was told I would be called to active duty for 6 months with the Army about 25 Feb.

21   Col. Chas. Clark, 5th Corps Area Quartermaster, approved my six months leave of absence to go to Alabama.

23   Received my transfer to the Air Corps Reserve.

24   Submitted application for active duty with the Air Corps.

26   Stayed home tonite for a change. Sure nice. Wish it would occur more often.

March 1   I never saw anything like it. Up to Janie's home again tonite.

2   Received my commission in the Air Corps.

7   *Queen Elizabeth*, world's largest ship, arrives in NYC. Thank goodness Janie has stayed with me at home this week.

8   Russia and Finland sign peace pact.

25   Application for active duty with the Air Corps disapproved. No funds. Working in Mobilization Planning.

April 5   Winston Churchill made Great Britain's defense minister.

7   Nazi troops march into Denmark and Norway.

12   British attack Germans in Norway. Battle raging at sea. At Janie's home all day till midnight!

May 8   It sure is great to be able to stay at home once—as we did tonite and read and listen to the radio—AT HOME FOR A CHANGE!

10   Germany invades Belgium, Holland, and Luxembourg. Chamberlain resigns as England's prime minister.

12   To Janie's home 131 times in 253 days since married!

13   Winston Churchill now Britain's prime minister. I am to go to Camp Williams, Wis. August 10-30 on 2d Army Maneuvers.

16   Hitler invades France.

17   President Roosevelt asks for $1,185,000,000 for "defense."

May 18   Nazi within 70 miles of Paris.

20   National Defense Bill being rushed through Congress.

21   Congress gives green light. Sky is the limit on Defense Funds Bill. Hitler takes channel ports and cuts off 40% of allied forces.

23   War Department radiogram called for all Air Corps officers to report for active duty.

24   Hitler strikes at England. King George talks to his Empire. Congress wants 50,000 airplane program rushed. I received assignment to Central Air Corps Procurement District, Wright Field, Dayton, Ohio. English and Nazi troops grapple for channel ports.

26   FDR gives fireside talk about the war.

27   Italy prepares for war. I made application for active duty.

28   King Leopold of Belgium surrendered today.

29   Nazi take Calais, France.

30   Allies retreat from Dunkirk. FDR asks another billion dollars for defense.

June 2   Nazi bomb Lyons and Marseilles, France.

3   Nazi bomb Paris, nearly hit Ambassador Bullett. British troops evacuation from France, nearly complete. Nazi advance toward Paris.

4   FDR requests power to call out National Guard if needed.

5   My application for active duty forwarded with others to HQ AAF.

6   Mother wants to invest all her money in a home for my parents and Janie and I. What next?

10   Italy declares war on England and France. IL Duce makes a fiery speech. Nazi within 35 miles of Paris.

11   Nazi attack Malta. US House Military Affairs Committee wants to increase the Army by 400,000.

12   US sends war planes and equipment to allies. Air and naval battles in Mediterranean Sea.

13   Nazi take Paris. Janie's 24th birthday.

14   Paris falls to Nazi. Maginot Line attacked front and rear.

June 17   Of the past 17 evenings or days 13 have been spent at Janie's home!

18   Hitler and Mussolini draft armistice terms for France.

20   FDR names Stinson sec'y of war, Knox, sec'y of navy.

22   France signs armistice with Hitler.

25   France signs armistice with Italy.

27   Wilkie nominated on 6th ballot for president by GOP.

28   Russia takes Bessarabia from Rumania.

29   Russian troops march into Rumania.

July 1   New taxes for national defense start today.

9   Am to go to Camp Williams, Wis., 2nd Army Maneuvers, 5 Aug. on V Corps QM staff. Only Lt. on the general's staff.

11   Received confidential letter from the Industrial Planning Office, AAF Materiel Center, Wright Field, Ohio, about my availability for active duty.

15   I took over Fiscal Procurement of CCC, Corps Area QM today.

16   Received Order #99 for AD tour Camp Williams, Wis., 5 Aug.

17   FDR nominated by Democratic Convention for 3rd Term on 1st ballot.

18   Forwarded application for extended active duty to HQ USAF.

23   Britain rejects Nazi demand to surrender.

Aug. 5   Left 7 A.M. Camp Williams, Wis. with 2d Lt. Lloyd Le May, brother of General Curtis Le May. Radiator trouble en route.

9   Appointed adjutant, V Corps HQ Quartermaster.

12   Received War Department radiogram from 2nd Army, CG, 5th Corps Area directing me to AD at Wright Field, Ohio, 15 August. Major J. J. Firestone talked to Colonel Drysdale, chief of staff, HQ 5th Corps Area to keep me until maneuvers are over. He talked to HQ USAF about it.

Aug. 15   Received W.D. radiogram directing me to report to Wright Field 2 Sept. This is the first anniversary of our marriage!

16   My parents want to move in with us!

27   On maneuvers, rain—rain. Got Superior on my efficiency report.

30   Le May and I left for home. Stayed in Beloit, Wis. tonite.

31   Arrive home at 8 P.M.

CHAPTER II

HQ, ARMY AIR CORPS MATERIEL DIVISION AND WRIGHT FIELD, OHIO (LATER DESIGNATED AAF MATERIEL COMMAND)

The Air Corps Materiel Division was charged with all Air Corps procurement, research, engineering, development, production and inspection of aircraft and related equipment under contract at industrial plants and facilities throughout the country.

The Division was comprised of 184 officers of the Air Corps and about 5,000 civilian employees, mostly aeronautical, research and other engineers, technicians, procurement inspectors, administrative personnel and specialists.

It was comparable to any large corporation and industry and functioned as such. The Division had three Procurement District Offices, each strategically located in industrial areas throughout the country. Each of these offices directed the activities of a large field organization which maintains surveillance to assure contract compliance, quality control and production.

Wright Field has frequently been referred to as the nerve center and heart of the Air Corps.

In 1944 over 44,000 civilian employees were connected with the procurement activities of the AAF Materiel Command. In August 1943 the number of Air Corps officers at Wright Field increased to 2,067. The tremendous growth of the Air Corps is reflected in the amount of funds that was approved for Army aviation. In 1938 $67,308,374,000 was authorized while $23,655,998,000 in funds were approved in 1944. The total weight of airframes in pounds of military aircraft produced in 1939 was 6,600,000 while in 1943 667,000,000 pounds were produced. The Material Command can well be proud of its magnificent achievement *in the engineering procurement, inspection and production of Army Air Forces aircraft and equipment. Thirty cents of every US War Dollar was spent by the Army Air Forces.*

The article below from the October 19, 1995, issue of the Richmond Times Dispatch *reflects the great importance of Wright-Patterson Air Force Base to our national defense 50 years after the end of World War II.*

Envoys hope Wright stuff works

THE ASSOCIATED PRESS

DAYTON, Ohio — Wright-Patterson Air Force Base — the site of the next round of Bosnia peace talks — began as the Wright brothers' testing grounds and grew into a vast complex of offices, hangars and labs.

The base is a world away from the fighting in Bosnia but only a hour's flight from Washington.

State Department spokesman Nicholas Burns said Wright-Patterson was selected over Langley Air Force Base in Virginia, Offitt Air Force Base in Nebraska and the Naval War College in Newport, R.I., because it offered the best combination of facilities.

The Air Force's largest domestic base is a small city in itself, with 1,600 buildings, including dormitories, restaurants, and a 260-room hotel. The 8,145-acre base employs 22,000 military and civilian workers.

Wright-Patterson also is the largest Air Force research and development site, headquarters to a worldwide military logistics system and home to more than 100 Pentagon organizations. It is run by 21 generals.

Sept. 2   Pursuant War Department radiogram received while on duty at the 2nd Army Maneuvers in Wisconsin. I reported to Wright Field, Ohio, at 8 P.M. today. This is the first anniversary of our marriage.

3   I was interviewed by Lt. Colonel John Y. York, Jr., *[later major general]*, asst. administrative executive to the commander of the Division and adjutant of Wright Field. He said he wanted me to help him. He assigned me as asst. administrative executive, asst. adjutant, asst. operations officer, asst. provost marshal and chief of the Reserve officers branch. 184 officers are assigned to the Division.

4   Visited Colonel York at his home on the base tonite.

20   Visited Col. Oliver Echols, asst. chief, Materiel Division, and Col. George C. Kenney, technical executive, at their homes.

Sept. 27   Japan signs a 10 year pact with Nazi and Italy.

Oct. 1   Went on inspection trip with chief of the power plant and two FBI agents. We are increasing the guard force.

9   Elliott Roosevelt reported at 4 P.M. I have all his mail. A lot of very critical cards and letters. *[See part 1A, chapter VI.]*

10   All morning I took care of Captain Elliott Roosevelt, son of the president. I drove him to Patterson Field for physical exam.

12   Columbus Day. President Roosevelt visits the base. I was the first officer to see him enter as I was at the gate. *[See part IA, chapter VI.]* I was the first man to leave the field afterward.

14   Captain Roosevelt submitted his resignation because of the uproar over his appointment but General Echols rejected it. *[See part 1A, chapter VI.]*

16   Registration for 16 million men required under Selective Service Act.

23   Received letter from Major Jimmy Doolittle today. *[See part 1B, chapter VI.]* Wants officers and orders.

28   Italy attacks Greece. England sends ships to defend Greece.

Nov. 1   Col. John Y. York gave me a compliment supposedly behind my back but I heard it.

2   Bought a new 1941 red Chevy 5 pass. Coupe.

5   FDR elected to a third term.

8   Looks like US is in about the same situation it was in 1916.

14   Appointed personnel officer in charge of the Army Personnel Administration Center in addition to my other duties.

15   General Echols made chief of the AAF Materiel Division.

21   Hungary joins the Axis.

25   Lt. Morris Felder assigned to help me take over Reserve Unit.

29   Appointed Class A finance agent to pay enlisted men assigned here.

Nov. 30   Paid enlisted men $7000.00.

Dec. 4   Obtained another room for the Administration Center. Four enlisted men and a stenographer to help.

13   I shook hands with a pilot from Orlando, Fla. at noon and at 3:10 P.M. he had been killed in a plane crash.

29   FDR gives a fireside chat on "Defense."

1941

Jan. 1   I wonder what this year will bring forth. The most critical in the history of this country, the world and democracy. America faces its greatest crisis.

3   I took my first airplane ride with Captain Walter Wood in a B-18 to Cincinnati and Hamilton, Ohio. In the air 1 hour and 5 minutes as an observer.

6   FDR makes speech on "State of the Nation." Asks billions for defense. Peacetime war.

7   US gives all aid to Britain.

8   FDR asks 17 1/2 billion dollars for defense.

9   Germany puts pressure on Bulgaria. Britain takes Bardia, Libya from Italians.

10   America's greatest Defense Bill goes to Congress. The one to save the democratic way of life for mankind.

13   America is at last arising to realize that it must be the "Arsenal of Democracy." FDR stirs action.

20   FDR inaugurated to 3rd term. Democracy on stand for its life. Britain's Air Chief Marshal Sir Hugh Downing spoke to us at a meeting here today.

21   Worked till 8:30 P.M. Boy, am I tired. Phone calls, teletypes and interviews.

24   Major John Joyce said Colonel York said he'd rather have me than the other 30 2d lieutenants put together! Whoopie!

27   Colonel Alonzo Drake asked Colonel York for my release from Wright Field so he could make me executive officer of the Central Air Corps Procurement District under him. Colonel York turned him down.

Jan. 30 Hitler celebrates 8 years of Nazi power by saying he'd torpedo US ships if they attempted to haul goods to Britain.

31 Colonel York said he'd approve my request to go to the next class at the Army Industrial College.

Feb. 4 Land Lease Bill controversy very heated.

10 England breaks off relations with Rumania.

11 Representatives of the secretary of war's office came to see me today about Specialist Reserve Commissions.

12 Nazi move into Bulgaria by transport planes.

13 Japanese threaten to move into Dutch East Indies Area. Hitler summons Yugoslavia foreign minister to Berlin. France's General Petain meets with General Franco of Spain.

14 Japan threatens in the Far East. Australia gets ready. American residents in Shanghai ordered home.

16 Hitler gets ready to go thru Bulgaria to Greece. Things get desperate.

20 Air Force in Pacific to be expanded.

24 Colonel York detailed me to escort the remains of Captain Russell Montgomery to his home in Scottsburgh, Ind. A five hour drive. He was burned up in an airplane crash near Athens, Ohio. His mother and father told me to stay in his room in their home.

26 Had services at Funeral Home this P.M. I read the obituary of Captain Montgomery. Tonite I went to a small country church for a meeting. *[See part IF, chapter VI.]*

27 Went to Louisville, Ky. and picked up 1st Lt. John Willard Montgomery, M.D., Captain Russell Montgomery's brother. I stayed at the Funeral Home this evening. Lieutenant Montgomery was stationed at Ft. Hood, Texas and was delayed. In civilian life the lieutenant was a technical adviser to the producer of the "Dr. Kildare" TV Series.

28 We buried Captain Montgomery. I presented the US flag to his mother at the grave. A truly heartrending week for me. She gave me an afghan and a pair of the captain's cuff links. *[See part IF, chapter VI.]*

March 3	Colonel York kidded me about being gone all last week. Received $24.32 for mileage.
4	Bulgaria joins the Axis Powers.
6	New B-26 Martin Bombers arrive at adjoining Patterson Field.
7	Nazi on Greek border.
12	FDR asks $7 billion for Britain.
14	Balkans aflame. Turkey, Greece and Yugoslavia behind the eight ball. Hitler pushing for quick victory.
17	FDR made great talk on defense.
18	I teletyped HQ AAF to get Jimmy Stewart to WF when drafted into service. Colonel York to be assigned to HQ AAF Plans Division by 1 April *[later made major general]*.
19	Trying to get Jimmy Stewart, movie actor, to duty at WF for duty in Motion Picture Unit. *[See part 1C, chapter VI.]*
21	Colonel York received letter from Mrs. Montgomery thanking him and expressed their gratitude and appreciation for my courtesies to them.
23	Russia backs Turkey, Yugoslavia in turmoil.
26	US plans to produce 80,000 airplanes by 1943.
28	British pilots flying planes from WF Yugoslavia now has Pro-British government.
April 1	Colonel York said to order Lieutenant Dickson and Captain Pernack to take over my work while I attend the Army Industrial College 5 July for 3 months.
2	Girls in the office got in a fight. I had to break it up and lecture them.
5	Nazi invade Yugoslavia and Greece.
11	FDR opens Red Sea to US ships.
16	Lieutenant Hanson, Patterson Field, said he was going to try to get me as personnel officer for the HQ 50th AF Wing. Fifi Dorsey, movie actress, at Officers' Club tonite for dinner.
23	Submitted report to commander of WF and Materiel Division on the requirements for Air Corps Reserve officers. A total of 1,033.

April 24   CIO labor strikes all over US. Too bad this happens now.

27   Greece falls to Nazi. Churchill speaks to British.

28   Col. Chas. A. Lindbergh sends his resignation to sec'y of war. FDR critical of his speech. He seems to be a pacifist.

29   Lindbergh's resignation is accepted.

30   FDR extends Combat Zone Patrol and initiates Defense Bond sales. Nazi head for Egypt.

May 1   FDR takes over Axis ships. Nazi advance on Egypt. Senator Chas. Sawyer of Cincinnati, Ohio, member of the Democratic Committee, called me about his son Charles Jr. about flying. The boy is on the radio tonite.

5   FDR orders 500 bombers a month from OPM. Democracies must obtain air superiority. Hitler says he is going to win.

6   Senator Claude Pepper of Florida urges US to "get tough" with dictators and take over Canary and Azores Islands. I inspected a Nazi JU 88 Bomber at the field here today—it landed in England.

7   Secretary of War Stimson urges US naval action to help Britain.

9   Colonel York, now at HQ AAF, wired me to send him names of some high powered executives and asked me to select them. 300 British planes bomb Hamburg and Bremen.

12   Rudolph Hess, No. 2 Nazi party leader, landed in Scotland. Believed mental derangement cause of flight and crash.

13   Believe Hess left Germany to escape purge or to desert Nazi cause.

15   It is believed Hess was on a "Peace Mission" to England.

19   Italians in Ethiopia surrender to British.

20   Nazi attack Crete.

23   Joe Louis defeated Buddy Bear.

25   Nazi navy sinks British battleship *Hood.*

May 27   FDR declares Unlimited National Emergency. German battleship *Bismarck* sunk by British navy. FDR takes over Emergency Power. Britain to be backed to the hilt and US will resist all Axis domination in Western hemisphere.

29   Nazi occupy Greek Island of Crete.

June 4   To HQ AAF, Munitions Bldg. Washington, D.C. Conference with Colonel McCoy.

9   FDR signs order for Army to take over the North American Aircraft Plant. Lt. Colonel Branshaw of our Division took charge.

10   North American aircraft workers go back to work under army guard.

11   British attack in Syria.

16   Stalin gives in to Hitler who seeks wheat and oil from Ukraine. US seizes Nazi and Italian credits. Hitler sends 500,000 troops to Africa.

18   Nazi signs agreement with Turkey.

20   British attacking Damascus.

21   Hitler declares war on Russia.

23   Britain to help Russia against Germany.

24   Nazi advancing in Russia.

25   Finland attacks Russia.

27   Major Umstead took the new XB-19A up for its first flight. World's largest plane. *[See (Part 4 (18), chapter VI.]*

July 2   I issued office memo about girls taking too much time off during office hours.

7   FDR sends Navy to take over Iceland.

10   US Marines to go to Iceland. Nazi slowed down on Russian front.

11    $3 Billion more asked for US Navy.

15   Lieutenant Dickson and I went to Cincinnati Summer Opera and had our pictures taken for the *Cincinnati Enquirer* with the Portuguese leading lady.

July 17   Sent confidential letter to HQ AAF after seeing article in "Friday Magazine" about Allen A. Zoll, applicant for Specialist Reserve Commission. *[See part 4 (13), chapter VI.]*

18   Nazi 250 miles from Moscow, approaching Kiev. I talked with Wing Commander Little of the RAF in the Officers Club locker room. He brought down 22 Nazi planes.

24   Japan takes over Indo-China.

29   Russia holds Nazi at Smolenze. US and Britain apply economic restrictions on Japan.

31   20th Century Fox movie productions make movie about Wright Field.

Aug. 6   We moved into new larger office with my staff.

7   Japs getting ready to take Thailand.

12   Nazi pushing on toward Odessa. Japan mobilizing. House of Representatives passes bill retaining selectees and reservists another 18 months. France collaborates with Nazi.

18   Nazi take Nicholi on the Black Sea and surround Odessa.

20   Nazi 75 miles from Leningrad and on way to Odessa.

22   British and Russians are about to invade Iran to keep Nazi out.

25   British and US warn Japan to go no farther.

27   Assassin shot and wounded Pierre Laval, Premier of Vichy, France. *[Convicted and executed for treason 1944.]*

Sept. 2   Nazi within 16 miles of Leningrad. Churchill pleads for US aid by all out effort.

4   Nazi and Russia in death struggle for Leningrad.

5   US destroyers shot at by Nazi U boat.

8   Leningrad surrounded by Nazi.

9   Nazi sink US ship in Red Sea and Panamanian US ship in Atlantic.

10   British and Canadians take Spitzbergen.

11   FDR says US will maintain Freedom of the Seas at all costs and will shoot back at Nazi and Italians in our Defense Zone.

Sept. 16   US ships being escorted by US Navy.

18   Nazi have cut off Crimea and have Ukraine in a pocket. FDR seeks $6 Billion more.

19   Nazi capture Kiev.

20   Visited Captain Montgomery's parents in Scottsburg, Ind. and stayed in their hotel.

21   Breakfast and lunch with Mr. and Mrs. Montgomery. They gave me Russell's purple cuff links.

22   Bulgaria to join Germany against Russia.

24   US about to arm merchant ships. FDR to ask repeal of Neutrality Act.

Oct. 4   33 Russian aviators at Patterson Field *[adjoins Wright Field]*.

6   Nazi start two way attack on Moscow.

8   I have had three years in grade today. Due for 1st lieutenant. Papers went to HQ AAF today.

14   Colonel Miller, admin. executive to Division commander and commander of Wright Field approved my attendance at the Army Industrial College Jan. 1 Class.

16   Nazi are in Odessa. Japanese cabinet resigns. Military clique takes over. Nazi surround Moscow.

17   US ships in Asiatic waters ordered to neutral ports. US destroyer struck by Nazi torpedo.

18   Party at Cobana Bar at Broad-Lincoln Hotel, Col's, Ohio, celebrating my promotion to 1st lieutenant.

20   Nazi near Moscow. Congress argues on Neutrality Act revisions.

22   Nazi push to Rostov.

23   Nazi 35 miles from Moscow. US Congress passes 2nd Land Lease Bill. US Army to increase Air Force to 400,000— 3 fold increase.

26   Nazi take Kharkov.

27   Took Janie to Grant Hospital in Columbus. Rm. 527, 7 days at $6.25 per day.

29   Janie operated on 10:50 A.M. till 11:25 A.M.

Oct. 31	US Destroyer sunk off Iceland. Janie's throat sore.
Nov. 3	US requests Finland to stop fighting Russia.
6	Stalin asks for more aid from British.
7	Nazi slowed up by Reds' counter attacks, Stalin says. Nazi will fall in one year.
8	Took Janie home from hospital.
11	Nazi push toward Sevastopol.
12	Jap envoy on way to Washington for decision in regard to the Far East.
13	Colonel Miller to be relieved as commander of Wright Field and promoted.
14	Neutrality Act and Armed Ship Bill passed 214 to 196. Italians sink the *Ark Royal*.
15	US government and CIO in fight over coal strike.
18	Nazi take Kerch in Crimea.
20	I'm 31 today. Got 2 ties, 3 shirts. Thanksgiving Day. Up at 3 P.M.!
22	British attack in Libya, drive back Italians and Germans. French General Maxime Weygand ousted by Vichy government. Nazi take Rostov-on-Don.
23	Nazi push toward Caucasus oil fields. Colonel Mollders, Nazi air ace killed.
24	US troops move into Dutch Guinea, S.A.
25	Congress to pass strike prevention bill and working on inflation bill.
27	FDR talks to Jap envoy as last resort. Jap troops on Thailand border.
28	Colonel Schneeberger, chief of mobilization planning, said he would like to have me in his Section if I would like it after I finish the course at the Army Industrial College.
30	US Jap talks at explosive point. Nazi press Vichy.
Dec. 1	Reds take Rostov Jap-US relations tense. Reds hold on all fronts.

Dec. 4   Japs to answer US Note and rebuke it.

5   England declares war on Rumania, Hungary and Finland today.

7   Japan declares war on US, attacks Pearl Harbor, Manila, Guam and Wake Island. Sinks ships. Kill 1,000 troops. Invades Thailand. All men in US Army to report in uniform.

8   FDR speaks to Congress 12:30 P.M. Congress and FDR declare war as does Britain and other countries. Colonel Miller called conference in his office 8:30 A.M. 24 hour work shifts set up.

9   Enemy planes threaten Golden Gate, attack Manila. I will go on duty at midnight in addition to my day duty. Conference in Commander's Office 8 A.M. NYC and Seattle blacked out. 44 hour work week set up.

10   Worked from 11:20 P.M. last nite all nite and all day today till 4:30 P.M. Awful tired. Two British battleships sunk. Maybe two aircraft carriers sunk. Mad world!

11   Germany and Italy declare war on US and US declares war on them. US sinks Jap battleship, cruiser and destroyer. Terribly busy. Col. George Usher takes command of the base.

15   Wake and Midway Islands hold out. Hong Kong being attacked.

16   Hitler suffering a nervous breakdown, will go to Berchtesgarden. Japs use two-man subs. Reds pushing Nazi back. Japs take Guam.

17   US holds Philippines against Japs.

18   Lt. General Emmons, AC, takes over Hawaiian Command. US to conscript all men 29 to 44 for military service.

22   Japs attack Philippines in force.

23   Marshal Henri Pétain resigns as chief of state in France. Admiral Darlan takes over and will collaborate with the Nazi.

26   Churchill spoke to Congress today. Allies to take initiative in 1943, he says. Manila declared an open city. Nazi retreat.

27   Japs attack and bomb Manila after we declared it an open city. Nazi sending troops to Libya.

Dec. 29   Worked till 8:30 P.M. Will work New Year's Day. Nazi push to Spanish border.

30   Reds take Kerch in Crimea. Churchill says war to take three phases. Congressman demand separate Air Force. Lindbergh asks Gen. H. H. Arnold, Chief of AAF, for a job in the AAF. Wright Field equipment and facilities exceed $25,000,000 and Congress just approved a major portion of $34,000,000 for Wright Field expansion.

1942

Jan. 1   Major Simes got in a mess on teletype to OCAC. I had to leave on 4:55 P.M. train for Washington.

2   Ran all around Washington, OCAC, AGO and undersecretary of war's Office. Dinner at Army-Navy Club. To Captain Gale's home tonite near Fairfax.

3   Lunch at Mayflower Hotel with Capt. Ben Gale.

4   Took Yellow Fever shot.

5   Japs defeated in China battle. Worked till 8 P.M..

6   FDR addresses Congress on State of the Nation. Wants 185,000 planes, 125,000 tanks and $60 billion for armaments next year.

7   Japs push on. Nazi retreat. Reds push to Kharkov and Kerch. Rubber tires are rationed.

8   6° below zero. Car froze up. Cost $100.00 to fix it. Lieutenant Pease sick from typhoid shot. Japs press on in Philippines.

9   Reds advance. Japs press toward Singapore.

12   6 day work week begins. Got typhoid shot.

13   Sick. Nearly died from effects of typhoid and yellow fever shots today.

15   Sec'y of War Stimson announces 3,600,000 army for 1942. Congress passes daylight saving time.

16   Aussies attack Japs in Malaysia. US Navy sinks 5 more Jap ships. 9 Lt. colonels made colonel. Knudsen made Lt. General, chief of Army production.

17   Carole Lombard killed in plane crash.

Jan. 18 Sunday. At office 7:40 A.M. Worked till 8 P.M. tonite.

19 Worked on report till 11 P.M.

20 Took manpower report to HQ OCAC, Washington.

21 Lt. A. K. Lovett and wife took me to dinner and then we went to Bolling Field Officers' Club for drinks.

22 Capt. John Gerrish and his wife took me to wharf front for seafood dinner. Then to his room in basement of a private home to sleep.

23 All day conference in Military Personnel Division, Office, Chief of Air Corps with manpower problems. Took 625 P.M. train to Dayton.

24 US Navy sinks 2 Jap ships. B-19 arrives at WF.

26 US troops land in Ireland. Went all thru B-19. World's largest plane. *[See (18), part 4, chapter VI.]*

27 Sugar to be rationed.

28 Navy voted $20,000,000, Army $12,000,000.

29 US fights Nazi subs off east coast. Japs 30 miles from Singapore.

30 FDR's 60th B/D. Japs demand McArthur surrender. Hitler says U boats to open up in the Atlantic.

Feb. 2 Japs press Far East drive. Nazi advance in Libya.

3 Singapore fighting to stave off Jap invasion.

12 Nazi big ships ran the Dover strait today. British lost 40 planes. Nazi lost 18 planes. Japs press on Singapore and Java.

15 Singapore surrenders to Japan. Worked all day on promotions and tables of organization.

17 Japs move on Java and Bataan. Nazi sink tankers in Atlantic.

19 Found an apt. in Osborn. Major Garvey took me to dinner. He won $53.00 on the slot machine.

20 Japs take Java and Bali. Reds push Nazi back in Latvia.

24 Japs cut Burma Road. Jap sub attacks Los Angeles-West Coast.

26 Rangoon burned by British and harbor area mined.

Feb. 27   Reds press on in Leningrad and Crimea area.

28   British troops make an attack on French Coast.

March 9   Lt. Gen. W. S. Knudsen, chief of US war production, was in our office today at 5-6 P.M. and he spoke to me about our manpower problems. Japs take Java and move toward Australia.

10   Japs take all of Indies and Nazi bomb Malta.

11   I held up the mail plane till our promotion list to go to OCAC was completed.

12   Reds attack Nazi in Ukraine.

13   Japs push toward Solomon Islands. Australia loses 2 cruisers.

20   Moved into our new apartment in Fairfield.

21   General MacArthur gets Congressional Medal of Honor.

27   RAF blasts Krupp munitions works in Germany.

30   18" snowfall in Wash., D.C.

31   Japs press on to Burma.

April 6   Shot up Jap plane on display here at the field.

8   Nazi start push in Africa. Japs press on to Bataan Peninsula.

9   Bataan Peninsula falls to Japs. Two British cruisers sunk by Nazi in Indian Ocean.

10   Promoted to captain. To rank from 1 March 1942.

17   RAF blasts French coast and Nazi factories. Reds press on toward Smolensk.

18   US planes attack Tokyo and Yokohama.

20   Chinese meet British in Burma.

21   Nazi forces push ahead in France and Norway.

22   Commandos raid French coast.

23   Hitler calls up 1,900,000 reserves.

28   FDR talks on radio on price controls and inflation.

May 2   Mandalay reported in Jap hands.

May 5   US prepares to equip 6,000,000 men in the Army.

6   Corregidor falls to the Japs. Got sugar ration cards.

7   French give up naval base on Madagascar.

8   US sink 17 Jap ships in Pacific area.

14   Reds push Nazi back from Leningrad. Gas rationing starts.

18   Reds surround Kharkov and hold Nazi in Crimea.

19   General Doolittle awarded Congressional Medal of Honor for attack on Tokyo. *[See part 1B, chapter VI.]*

21   Gas rationing by 1 July. Japs push on in China.

25   Reds and Nazi battle for Kharkov.

27   Marshal Rommel starts Nazi drive in Africa.

28   Nazi start drive in Libya. Rommel moves toward Egypt.

June 1   RAF sends 1,000 planes to Cologne and blasts three quarters of the cities to pieces.

4   General Doolittle at WF with Undersecretary of War Patterson and General Echols in my office.

5   Japs attack Midway Islands.

7   US Navy sinks Jap ships at Midway Islands.

10   Nazi pound Sevastopol.

12   US Aircraft carrier *Lexington* sunk by Japs in Coral Sea. Japs land in Aleutian Islands, Alaska.

18   Sevastopol and Tobruck about to fall.

19   FDR and Churchill discuss a second Front offensive.

21   Marshal Rommel takes Tobruck and heads for Egypt.

22   I am acting adjutant of WF for two weeks. Japs fire on west coast of US and Canada.

24   US ship losses tremendous due to Nazi U-boats.

25   Bremen, Germany set afire by 1,000 RAF bombers.

July 2   Sec'y of War Stimson, Asst. Sec'y of War Lovett and General Echols at WF for Glider demonstration.

3   Sevastopol falls to Nazi.

4   I was promoted to major.

July 8	Generals Marshall, Arnold, Andrews and Echols at WF today for an important conference.
9	Nazi push 2,000 tanks into Don River Basin for breakthrough. Glider show here at WF for Air Corps chief of staff.
17	Nazi within 75 miles of Rostov.
28	Nazi take Rostov.
Aug. 12	US Marines advance in Solomon Islands.
17	Churchill to see Stalin in Moscow.
19	British, French, Canadians and US Air Corps and troops land on French soil with tanks and heavy artillery in big commando raid.
21	British commandos get 95 Nazi planes on raid to Dieppe.
24	US lands big convoy in Britain.
27	Japs pounded in New Guinea and Solomons.
Sept. 1	A B-24 burned up on the field here today.
15	Stalingrad fighting for its life.
16	US loses aircraft carrier *Yorktown* to Jap attack at Midway.
23	I represented Colonel Brownfield, Wright Field commander, at presentation of Army-Navy "E" Award at Frigidaire Division, GMC, and reception at Biltmore Hotel, Dayton.
Oct. 21	M. J. Connelly of Senator Truman's Senate Committee and I spent the P.M. studying the Production Control Section of the Production Division of the Command.
23	French fortify Dakar, West Africa, with 500 planes.
24	Allies open offensive in Africa. Colonel Rickenbacker lost in Pacific ocean.
25	J. E. Campbell, 1430 Bluss St., Zanesville, Ohio called me. He said seven airplanes flew over the cemetery yesterday where his little boy was buried. He loved aviation. A great coincidence.
31	Japs retreat from Guadalcanal.

Nov. 3	News that Clark Gable might be assigned to the base stirs up all the women here.
4	US troops arrive in Asia Minor.
7	US opens up second front offensive by invading West Africa in force. General Eisenhower in command.
10	US advance in Tunisia. I stopped a black/white girl fight in my office.
11	Nazi troops rush through unoccupied France to Marseilles and Toulon.
14	Col. Eddie Rickenbacker found in Pacific.
16	US troops advance in Tunisia.
17	US wins naval battle in Solomon Islands.
18	Held meeting with Generals Wolfe, Carroll and Base Commander Colonel Brownfield. Draft deferments for government employees are eliminated.
22	Nazi retreat in Caucasus and around Stalingrad.
24	I led Bob Hope and his group thru the crowd to a hangar on the flight line for a performance for all the personnel on the base.
27	French scuttle ships as Nazi take Toulon.
29	Reds have Nazi on the run at Stalingrad.
Dec. 1	US pushes ahead in New Guinea, Africa and Solomons.
4	FDR kills WPA. WF plant and facilities exceed $200,000,000.
7	One year of war and we are getting ahead on all fronts. US production up and on the way.
8-9	Worked hard and late on 1943 officer requirements report for the Materiel Command.
10	RAF bombers knock out industrial targets in Turin, Italy.
14	Marshal Rommel retreats to Tunisia.
18	All passenger car rations stopped on the east coast.
21	Nazi on retreat in Russia and Tunisia.
24	French Admiral Darlan assassinated in Africa.
27	General Giraud succeeds Admiral Darlan as the French leader.

Comedienne Phyllis Diller, the author's cousin, was often a member of Bob Hope's group of entertainers that put on shows for thousands of service men and women at various times and places.

1943

Jan. 2   US sinks seven Jap ships. Reds advance on all fronts.

7   FDR opens 78th Congress. He says we'll advance in 1943 and are assured of victory.

8   I have a staff of 31 people now.

10   US push Japs back in New Guinea. Rommel nearly trapped in Africa.

Jan. 12   Reds have the Nazi on the run in Caucasus.

18   RAF blasts Berlin with 4 ton Block Busters.

21   Members of the US Eagle Squadron in England here telling of their experiences.

26   In Promotion Board Meeting. Interviewed 75 officers.

27   Have 3 more officers under me now. Total of 7 and a warrant officer on the way.

31   I worked from 9:30 A.M. to 6 P.M. on 1943 overall officer requirements. FDR returns from Casablanca Conference with Churchill. All troops around Stalingrad liquidated.

Feb. 1   I now supervise eight officers and twenty-eight others in my office.

3   Japs attempt to retake Guadalcanal. Reds push ahead to Rostov.

8   Shoes are rationed—3 pair per year.

9   My boss, Col. Geo. Usher, WF Commander, promoted to brig. general. His picture was in *Life* magazine with Eddie Rickenbacker in Samoa.

13   US to draft 12,000 men daily.

15   Reds take Rostov. Nazi battle US troops in Tunisia.

16   When day is done I'm really fagged out. Kharkov falls back into Red hands.

18   US troops retreat in Tunisia.

19   Madam Chiang Kai-shek addresses Congress.

22   FDR makes fireside chat tonite. Washington's birthday.

23   Ghandi on 21 day "fast." Paint rationing begins.

24   Marshal Rommel forced back in Tunisia.

26   Col. Alfred Howse, asst. technical executive to the commander, asked me again about going out to one of the procurement districts in any job I wanted.

29   Germany now bombed 24 hours a day.

March 3   Nazis give up Rheza to Reds. Berlin bombed heavily.

4   Japs lose 22 ships in convoy by our air attack.

March 8	As a member of our Officer Candidate Review Committee we interviewed 102 men for possible assignment to Officer Candidate School.
9	Interviews and reports go to Colonel Brownfield, WF C.O. and General Vanaman, Materiel Center Commander.
10	FDR proposes a Post War Security Plan.
11	Rommel retreats. Nazi try to take Kharkov.
12	Meat, fish and butter to be rationed 1 April.
15	Reds advance and US pushes ahead in Africa.
17	Nazi take Kharkov.
18	American production on the upbeat.
19	Gen. "Hap" Arnold, AF chief, to be made full general.
20	About 47 of our colonels will be transferred within the next 90 days.
22	Butter, lard and fats to be rationed.
23	US and British forces corner Marshal Rommel.
24	Post War Planning is studied. Nazi retreat in Tunisia.
25	General Vanaman and Colonel Brownfield are fussing.
26	In conference all day.
27	Big reorganization of AAF. Our General Echols to command Materiel, Air Service Command and Air Transport Command.
28	Worked all day interviewing Wright Field civilian employees, mostly engineers for commission.
29	To boxing matches tonite for benefit of Wright Field enlisted men's athletic equipment.
30	General Branshaw from Western Procurement District to command AAF Materiel Command. Gen. Arthur Vanaman transferred to Air Service Command at Oklahoma Air Depot.
April 1	100 B-17 bombers hit Sardinia bases.
3	Brought a hoe to use in my victory garden.
6	US planes blast Naples and Rommel.

April 9   Nazi on the run in Tunisia. RAF blasts Ruhr Valley continually. General Branshaw cleaning house and shaking down the command. FDR sets up price levels.

10   Colonel Brownfield relieved as administrative executive and Col. "Spike" Eckert succeeds him and is my new boss. He's tough *[later lieutenant general]*.

13   Senator Truman's Committee representative here.

15   US and British tighten ring around Tunis. US and RAF hit Stuttgart, Germany.

16   Conference all P.M. with Colonel Eckert, Colonel Crawford and General Branshaw on policy matters.

17   Gen. Branshaw wants reports and more reports.

18   SUNDAY. Worked all day till 6 P.M. on officer reports for Gen. Branshaw.

19   Gen. Branshaw reorganizing. Four more procurement districts to be established.

26   To Mitchell Field, N.Y. for HQ AAF Personnel Conference.

27   Received commendation from Colonel Brownfield, commander, Wright Field. FDR having trouble with John L. Lewis, head of UMW's striking miners. US take over mines and troops to guard them.

May 4   US troops advance toward Bizerte. Colonel Brownfield leaves for Australia.

6   Colonel Robbins made commanding officer of WF.

7   Colonel Goddard has big write-up in *Life* magazine.

8   Tunis and Bizerte surrender to US and British troops.

10   25,000 Nazi troops surrender to Yanks in Tunisia.

11   Churchill arrives in Washington for conference re invasion of Europe.

13   180,000 Axis troops surrender in Tunisia.

14   US troops attack Japs at Attu in Alaska.

17   Nazi dams in Ruhr Valley bombed.

19   Churchill pledges Congress that Britain will fight Japs with us after Nazi are beaten.

23   Worked in victory garden all day.

May 24   RAF drop 200 tons of bombs in Dortmund in Ruhr Valley.

25   General Branshaw inspected WF troops.

27   Rained every day this month.

28   Conference in General Branshaw's office with him and Charles A. Lindbergh.

30   Memorial Day. Worked all day in garden.

31   US troops take Attu from Japs.

June 1   John L. Lewis' coal miners are striking again.

5   US aircraft bomb Italy.

14   Allies blast Italy and Sicily by air.

15   Nazi moving population to Eastern Germany.

16   Italy and Germany heavily bombed from the air.

18   Colonel Eckert gave me "Superior" rating while serving under him.

21   Moved into new larger office in Museum building.

22   Col. H. Y. Smith my new boss. He was in personnel with Shell Oil Co. in SF before the war.

23   Victory garden doing well. RAF blasts Italy and Germany.

25   Allies bomb Greece.

28   Congress passes anti-strike bill.

29   In Promotion Board meeting 10 A.M. to 3 P.M. Worked in office 7-11 P.M. tonite.

July 1   Col. Russell Keillor, commanding officer, Ladd Field, Alaska, requested that I be assigned to the command as his executive officer.

2   Gen. C. E. Branshaw and Gen. L. T. Miller made major generals. US flyers win big air battle in New Georgia Islands in Pacific.

4   US defeat Japs in naval battle.

6   Col. Alonzo Drake, district superior, Midcentral Procurement District, Chicago, Ill., wants me to head up his personnel program in Chicago.

July 7   I worked on a project for Col. Al Crawford, technical executive to the commanding general, till 9:30 P.M. *[later brigadier general]*.

9   Eight men killed at the field today in a two plane air collision.

11   Allies advance 100 miles in Sicily.

12   Allies press on in Sicily and take Syracuse.

13   Relieved as chief, military personnel and will study civilian personnel activities until I leave for duty in Chicago 15 August per request of Colonel Drake.

15   Worked on board proceedings on officer reassignments.

17   Executive Promotion Board meeting all day.

21   Allies occupy half of Sicily.

23   US 7th Army under Gen. Geo. Patton take Palermo, Sicily.

25   Leaving tonite for Washington. HQ AAF Personnel Conference.

26   Mussolini resigns as Italian Premier. King Emanuel and Gen. Pietro Badoglio take over.

28   FDR talks about war on the radio tonite.

30   Riots all over Italy.

31   Mussolini under guard. Allies reject Badoglio's peace terms.

Aug. 2   Capt. W. P. Lester and Lt. Col. J. E. Davis killed in air crash this eve.

5   British take Catania, Sicily and Reds take Orel, Russia.

6   Talked with Col. Elliott Roosevelt again. He is just back from Africa.

12   Col. H. Y. Smith gave me an "Excellent" report and told me about my new job in Chicago.

15   Left for my new assignment in Chicago. Staying at the North Shore Hotel.

16   Reported to Austin Bldg., 111 W. Jackson Blvd., next to Board of Trade Bldg. HQ, Midcentral Procurement District, Chicago. Assigned as district civilian personnel officer.

CHAPTER III

HQ, ARMY AIR FORCE MIDCENTRAL PROCUREMENT DISTRICT,
111 W. JACKSON BLVD., CHICAGO, ILL.

*The functions of the Army Air Corps Materiel Division were described
in chapter II. The Air Corps Materiel Division was redesignated AAF
Materiel Command on 9 March 1942.*

*The Materiel Command established six AAF procurement districts
throughout the US. Each district was assigned the responsibility for
maintaining surveillance over the procurement contracts, production
and inspection of aircraft and related equipment at plants and facilities
within its region. Under the district supervisor, and his staff, these functions
were performed through area offices, sub-offices, AAF resident
representatives and/or inspectors in charge at industrial plants and facilities.
The following map shows the area and sub-area offices in the
five states comprising the Midcentral Procurement District. On 1 June
1944 there were about 250 Air Force officers and 4,000 civilian employees
on duty in the district.*

*The scope and impact of the procurement activities of the AAF
Midcentral Procurement District is succinctly stated in the following
Chicago newspaper articles:*

The employees in the aircraft plants and facilities, working with personnel of the AAF Materiel Command, put together the sinew and core of the mightiest airforce in the world. The air power thus created was a dominant factor that resulted in the total defeat of the Axis Powers.

General Dwight D. Eisenhower put it in perspective when he said, "Our Home Fronts have given us an overwhelming superiority in weapons and munitions of war."

Upon activation of this district and my assignment to duty, I activated, planned, organized and established a completely decentralized district organization for civilian personnel management covering five states. With seven operating personnel offices we were the most decentralized of all the six districts. We received compliments on our operations, and although the district had 25% of all the No. 1 critical labor shortage areas in the US and in three war manpower regions, three civil service regions, and three service commands, we did pretty good despite these handicaps.

In May 1944 I was promoted to district personnel officer and assistant administrative executive to the district supervisor.

AIR FORCES PROCURE- MENT CHIEF—Col. Alonzo M. Drake.

THE chief of the Central Procurement District for the Army Air Forces in Chicago is Col. Alohzo M. Drake, a short, fiery officer of the regular Army who has the reputation among manufacturers and military men of getting things done.

He is proud to say of himself that people can come to him and "be sure to get an answer— quickly!"

Col. Drake was placed in charge of the Detroit area at a time when the automobile manufacturers were converting their huge industries to war production. Having gotten this program under way, the colonel was moved to Chicago to head one of the largest Air Force procurement districts in the country.

Air Forces Contracts Here Set at $2,400,000,000

Army Supervisor Reveals Midwest's Part in Supplying Invasion Needs

The part that Chicago and the five Midwestern states of Illinois, Indiana, Wisconsin, Minnesota and Iowa are playing in creating an air umbrella for the invasion of Europe and the battles with Japan was outlined yesterday by Col Alonzo M. Drake, district supervisor for the material command of the Army Air Forces.

Approximately 200,000 of the 445,000 men and women employed on Air Forces contracts in the five-state district are employed in the Chicago area, Col. Drake said. Contracts now in force in the district call for an expenditure of $6,000,000,000, with Chicago doing $2,400,000,000 worth of this work.

The Midcentral Procurement District, under command of Col. Drake, was established here in July, 1943. Since then, the colonel said, his office has purchased approximately $165,000,000 worth of aircraft equipment.

About $19,000,000 worth of this equipment, covering thousands of items, has been purchased in Illinois, he said.

"The new year, which will find the Army Air Forces on the offensive on every front in this global struggle, must find the Army Air Forces production on the offensive," Col. Drake declared.

Women work on aircraft at production plant. (OWI)

The output of aircraft in 1944 must be increased 75 per cent over the production of 1943 and 26 per cent above the production rate of the last quarter of 1943, he added.

On the basis of the rapid strides made in converting Midwestern corn field sites into aircraft production centers, the colonel predicted that "this section of the country will continue to occupy an important place in the aviation industry."

Aug. 19	Played golf with Major Harry Smith at Edgewater Golf Club.
22	Went thru Chicago Art Institute and Grant Park. At Hotel Maryland tonite.
23	Left for Indianapolis.
24	To our area office and to Allison Engine Plant.
Sept. 3	Moved into my new apartment. US invades Italy and advance.
5	Took cruise on Lake Michigan to Benton Harbor, Mich.
7	Personnel Conference all day.
8	Italy surrenders to Allies.
10	Nazi take Rome and battle allies in Northern Italy. Captain Dollison, my assistant, in his room all day in a drunken condition.
13	Nazi parachutists "free" Mussolini.
14	Had War Bond Rally in my office. *[See chapter VI.]*
15	War Bond Rally on 43rd floor Civic Opera Bldg.
16	Made staff visit to our Milwaukee area office. Dinner with Col. Walter Bain.
17	Rode in coach on train to our Minneapolis area office. Dinner with Major Edgar at Clarkes.
18	Left for Indianapolis office and Ft. Wayne, Ind. via Chicago to Evansville, Ind. Train packed with troops. Arr. 8:30 P.M.
19	Went to Republic Aviation Plant and looked over its production layout in making P-47 aircraft. Left for Indianapolis area office and sub-office in Ft. Wayne, Ind.
20	Staff visit to sub-office in Ft. Wayne, Ind. Arrived at 3 A.M. Went to a talk in the Chamber of Commerce Bldg. by Colonel Love on aircraft production. Left with Colonel Mechlin for South Bend.
21	Went to four hotels in South Bend and no rooms were available. Ran into Navy shore patrol and Ensign Charles L. Bryner of Pa. put me up in his hotel room with him. He had orders to sea duty.
22	Visited our South Bend Area Office with Colonel Mechlin and Major Don Eddy at the huge Bendix Plant.

Sept. 23   Nazi retreat to Dneiper and burn Naples.

25   Worked till 10 P.M. Area and Resident Representative Conference.

25   Gave a talk to area and resident representatives and inspectors in charge at conference. HQ, AMC officers talk.

28   Received letter of commendation from Major Gen. James M. Bevans, HQ, AAF for my work last June on the AAF personnel data system. *[Awarded Army Commendation Medal.]*

29   Allies advance in Italy and New Guinea. Got my gas ration book.

30   Nazi driven from Naples and back of Dneiper River. Big investigation at AAF Central Air Procurement District over the sale of $2,000,000 worth of tools for $70,000.

Oct. 1   US 5th Army enters Naples.

9   US planes bomb cities deep in Germany.

11   Reds near Kiev.

12   Nazi raze Kiev.

13   Italy declares war on Germany.

19   All Procurement District Personnel Officers' Conference at Wright Field.

20   Returned to Chicago on P.R.R. The dirtiest train I ever saw.

21   MCPD Promotion Board meeting.

22   Secretary of State Hull, British Foreign Minister Eden, confer with Red Foreign Minister Molotov in Moscow.

24   US planes attack Germany from Italy.

25   US aircraft blast 130 more Jap planes in Rabad.

27   FDR recommends all service men be given one year college work after the war.

30   Hull, Eden and Molotov reach agreement in Moscow.

Nov. 1   540,000 coal miners strike and FDR orders US to take over mines. USSR, US, Grt. Britain and China agree on Post War Plans. Badoglio demands King Emmanuel of Italy abdicate.

Nov. 2	In Detroit on business at Central Procurement District.
4	Thirty cents of every US war dollar is spent by the Army Air Forces.
6	Reds take Kiev. Nazi trapped in Ukraine and Crimea. US Senate approves World Peace Organization.
8	Hitler says Germany in dire peril. Reds advance closer to Polish border. Stock market slumps in "Peace Talk."
9	Hitler says he'll fight to the finish. Churchill says Germany's done for but many casualties will occur.
12	Had all five of my area office civilian personnel officers in for a conference. Colonel Drake, our district supervisor, complimented us on our work.
13	With friends, saw Notre Dame beat N.W.U. 25 to 6. Reds advance within 60 mi. of Poland.
14	Badoglio to resign as soon as Allies take Rome. US planes sink many Jap ships in New Britain Pacific waters.
16	Personnel problems are filled with psychology and no two alike. Looks like inflation is near.
18	Went to pistol firing range on top of Federal Reserve Bldg. and shot .45 cal. pistol. Spent P.M. at the Dodge Chicago plant, largest in the world, 84 acres in one bldg.
19	US bombs Berlin again with 1,000 planes. Berlin devastated.
22	US attacks Japs in the Gilbert Islands.
23	General Patton strikes soldier in Sicily and apologizes.
24	Berlin bombed three nights in a row. 25,000 casualties.
25	US takes Gilbert Islands and attacks Marshall Islands.
27	Visited the Buick aircraft engine plant. Enormous facility. Produces 3,000 engines a month. They are going to lay off 2,500 employees.
28	Went to a dance at the Medinah Club. Home at 3 A.M.
29	Visited the Studebaker Plant. Went thru Cicero, the tough town adjoining Chicago. Berlin bombed fifth night in a row.
30	Manpower problems are our major concern. FDR, Churchill, Chiang-Kai-Shek meet in Cairo for conference and go to Iran to meet Stalin. 1,029 marines killed in Tarawa in 76 hours and take the Gilbert Islands.

Dec. 5 We spent the P.M. in the Field Museum of Natural History on Lake Shore Dr. Wonderful exhibits.

6 Teheran conference in Cairo announces that Turkey will aid allies "short of war."

8 US force down 75 Jap planes and sink 2 destroyers in New Britain area. Working late every nite.

9 Manpower representative from the War Dept. Manpower Board will visit us for a couple of weeks starting the 13th.

11 I held a Personnel Officers' Conference. I have now planned, organized and activated five area office personnel offices over which we establish policies, programs, procedures and maintain surveillance. These offices are in Minneapolis, Milwaukee, Chicago Area, South Bend and Indianapolis.

13 War Dept. Manpower Board representative visited our office to review our workload analysis. Left with Major Jack Morton tonite at 815 P.M. for Wichita, Kans.

14 Train to Wichita 2 1/2 hrs. late. Arr. 3 P.M. Two day conference with staff of the AAF Midwestern Procurement District.

16 Train 6 hrs. late. Got into berth at 5 A.M. up at 10:10 A.M. On train all day. Arr. Chicago 6:15 P.M.—8 1/2 hrs. Late. 21 cars on train.

20 Yanks blast Bremen again. Capt. Jimmy Stewart on raid.

21 I presented the Distinguished Flying Cross Medal to the mother of S/Sgt. Anthony J. Rauba, Chicago Heights, Ill. He participated in the Ploesti oil fields bombing raid and is a Nazi prisoner in Bulgaria. *[See part 2B, chapter VI.]*

22 US 8th Air Force bomb Germany 7th time this month. 500,000 casualties expected in 3 mos.

24 FDR makes Xmas eve fireside chat on world affairs.

26 Nazi battleship *Shornhorst* sunk by British.

27 FDR orders Sec'y of War Stimson to take over the railroads at 6 P.M. tonite. CIO chief calls off steel strike.

30 US flyers destroy 57 Jap planes in New Britain. General Eisenhower takes command in London. Reds break 185 mile hole in Nazi lines. 300,000 Nazi troops are imperiled. Yankees take Gloucester air base in New Britain.

Dec. 31　Staff visit to our Milwaukee office.

1944

Jan. 1　Believe Germany will collapse this year. Reds 38 mi. from Polish border. Wonder if I will be in Chicago a year from today! *[No, I was in Oakland, Calif.]*

3　Destroyer explodes off New York. RAF blasts Berlin 10th time. Hitler's chancellory blown to pieces.

4　Reds inside old Polish border. 2,600 allied planes blast French coast. US troops advance on New Guinea.

6　Staff visit to Minneapolis area office and St. Paul Modification Center. Mississippi River frozen over.

10　Chicago to Wright Field on business.

12　Saw German JU-88, ME 109-F aircraft and our B-29 bomber at the hangar at WF

13　Staff visit to Indianapolis area office.

14　Moved our office to larger offices on second floor. I now have the best private office in the bldg.

15　War Bond Rally at Chicago Area Office.

16　Reds open Leningrad drive.

17　Busy on 4th war bond drive as War Bond officer.

19　Colonel Salsman, district supervisor, gave me a check for $1,125.00 for $1,500.00 War Bond at HQ rally.

20　Staff visit to Dodge Plant on personnel problems.

21　Busy with War Bond rallies with Major Harry Olson who was 16 months in Africa, Sicily, Italy, India and China.

22　To Central Procurement District in Detroit for War Bond Rally and talks on deferment policies.

24　I made a presentation of the Air Medal to the wife of 2d Lt. Roy Stealey, Harvey, Ill., before the Rotary Club Luncheon meeting. Her husband is a prisoner of the Nazi. *[See part 2B, chapter VI.]*

25　Awful busy on War Bond Campaign. The 4th War Loan is the biggest yet. US troops 23 miles from Rome.

26　Bought War Bonds. Showed war film "Baptism of Fire" to employees. Yanks blast Rabaul.

28　66% of US Armed Forces to go overseas.

Jan. 29 US planes blast Frankfurt and Berlin with 3,000 aircraft. Jap atrocities arouse US

30 Visited Chicago Natural History Museum.

31 Staff visit to Bendix Victor Adding Machine and Doughlas Plants on personnel problems.

Feb. 1 Major Harry Olson, who had 16 mos. overseas, and I went to Milwaukee Area Office and talked to graduation class of Trainee Inspectors at the Vocational School and to 200 people of the Milwaukee Area Office at the War Bond Rally with the Army Orchestra and entertainers provided.

2 US Marines, Navy and 7th Infantry take Marshall Islands. Reds enter Estonia.

6 Visited Chicago Aquarium and Planetarium. 300,000 Nazi troops trapped by Reds in South Russia. US takes over Marshall Islands.

8 All day in Conference with Area Personnel Officers at Milwaukee Vocation School and area office. We toured the school and its operation reviewed.

9 Continued CPO conference. Colonel Salsman, the District Supervisor, called a War Bond Rally at 2 P.M. for all HQ officers.

11 Nazi attack allies on beachhead south of Rome. Reds advance deeper in Ukraine.

15 HQ conference of all AAF resident plant representatives. They all griped about their personnel problems.

16 Attend District Employee Welfare Assoc. Dance.

17 RAF blasts Berlin—2,800 tons of bombs—largest drop yet. Colonel Salsman and I went to Wright Field on business.

18 Anzio beachhead in Italy in danger.

20 US naval aircraft sink 19 Jap ships and down 201 Jap planes at Truk. US holds Anzio beachhead in Italy, 1,000 planes blast Germany's fighter plane plants.

21 2,000 US planes blast Germany. Jap General Tojo fires his Army and Navy chief of staff and announces losses at Truk.

Feb. 22 Arrived in Evansville, Ind. Spent 2 hours going thru Sarvel, Inc. plant of 80 acres where they make wings for the P-47 fighter aircraft. Had to stay in a private home last nite.

23 Interviewed ordnance female inspectors for Chicago at the Republic P-47 plant at Evansville, Ind. Spent two hours in Terre Haute en route home.

25 Busy as a bee. Driving me nuts with major problems all at once. US bag 125 Jap planes.

26 HQ office bowlers all went to Milwaukee in a special train car and diner to compete with Milwaukee office bowlers. Arr. back in Chicago 3:40 A.M.

28 Colonel Finkenstadt and I visited the Chicago area office with Lt. Jim Lynch on the manpower and deferment problem. Chicago goes into a Group 1 Labor Area—critical.

March 1 Several meetings held on deferments and problem of authorization of 200 inspectors.

2 Jim Mahoney of the Civil Service Commission and I went to confer with Dean Spencer, the War Manpower Commission's regional director to clear radio publicity. Colonel Finkenstadt and I went to our South Bend, Ind., area office and the Studebaker Plant to discuss deferment problems.

3 My commander, Colonel Salsman, and I went to the 6th US civil service regional office for conference on manpower problems. Colonel Finkenstadt and I went to our Milwaukee area office for conference on manpower and deferment problems.

6 US planes blast Berlin and we lose 68 bombers and 20 fighter planes. 178 Nazi fighter planes downed.

8 2,000 US planes again attack Berlin.

9 Left for Chanute Field, Rantoul, Ill. with Lt. Orville Schmidt of the production office of the Chicago area office to try to recruit personnel for the plants in the Chicago area. It was a successful trip.

10 Spent the day at Navy pier with our people and Jim Mahoney of the 6th U.S.C.S. region, signing up Navy instructors for inspection activities at the Douglas Plant and other facilities in our district.

March 14 Spent the day at Chanute Field, Ill., with Jim Mahoney, 6th U.S.C.S. region, recruiting. Met with the commander, Brigidier General O'Neil.

15 US Bombers destroy Cassino, Italy. Reds advance to Rumania border. Japs pounded on Solomons and New Guinea.

16 Jim Mahoney, 6th U.S.C.S. region, and I went to the Dodge plant, 84 acres under one roof—the world's largest plant.

17 All day conference on personnel problems with Colonel Salsman, district supervisor, and Capt. James Gaylord, HQ AAF materiel command personnel liaison officer.

18 Manpower is the nation's and my biggest problem now.

19 2,000 US Bombers attack Germany. Finland refuses peace approaches by Russia. Allies take Cassino, Italy.

20 Another 1,000 planes bomb Germany.

21 Lt. Gen. George Patton relieved of command of the 7th US Army.

22 1,500 US planes raid Berlin 5th time this week. Nazi take over military rule of Hungary.

24 Nazi take over Bulgaria, Hungary and Rumania. 1500 US planes blast Germany. I had all the area personnel officers in my office for a meeting.

26 Churchill talks on radio. Big battle in Burma.

29 Reds advance in Rumania. 4 F draftees to be put in war work or drafted. I worked at home till midnite.

April 1 Arguments on reclassification of positions. I'm fed up with the whole set-up. Wish I could get overseas. Worked till 8 P.M.

2 Sun. Got up at 6 P.M. Wrote a lot of letters all over the world.

3 Left on NYC Limited train for NYC to attend a HQ, AAF Personnel Mgt. Conference. Maj. Gen. J. M. Bevans and General Adler gave talks. Discussions on personnel problems. To movie to see "Winged Victory."

6 I saw the repatriation ship *The Gripsholm* in the Hudson River.

7 Another day of conference. Colonel Conover, Captain Gaylord and I went to Roxy Theatre to see Harry Richmond. US sink 28 Jap ships.

April 8   Conference ends at noon. Went to HQ, EPD at 67 Broad St. Saw Colonel Hutchins and others.

10   My father is stationed at the AAF Convalescent Hospital, St. Petersburg, Fla.

13   2,000 US planes blast Germany.

16   To a Tea Dance at the ballroom of the Knickerbocker Hotel with Major and Mrs. Harry Olson.

17   An insurance man jumped from the 18th floor of the Board of Trade Bldg. across the street, to his death. He couldn't get help! *[See part 2D, chapter VI.]*

18   2,000 US planes blast Germany but lose 116 bombers. Reds take Crimea. Capt. Manuel Siwek from Wright Field to relieve me as district civilian personnel officer and I am to be promoted to asst. admin. executive and district personnel officer.

19   2,000 US planes bomb Nazi Europe. England is an arsenal.

24   3,000 allied planes bomb invasion coast.

27   To Milwaukee area office. US government takes over Montgomery Ward & Co., and police carry out the chairman of the board of directors from his office.

28   Secretary of the Navy Knox died.

29   We moved into our new apartment overlooking Lake Michigan.

30   Again, 2,000 US planes blast invasion coast.

May 1   498 US troops lost in ship transporting troops. Again, 2,000 US planes blast invasion coast.

2   Attended meeting of Federal Personnel Council of Chicago. Invasion coast blasted daily.

7   SUNDAY. Up at 10:30 A.M. We got a garden for $7.00 already worked. 14' x 24', 100 yards from Lake Michigan and 100 yards from our apartment. We planted vegetables.

9   7,000 US planes blast invasion coast the past two days.

10   To Wright Field on business trip.

13   Capt. Manuel Siwek reported today. He takes my job. I am promoted to district personnel officer and asst. admin. executive to the district supervisor. Major "Dick" Bong, Pacific area Ace flyer who shot down 26 Jap planes talked to me.

May 14   Played golf at Edgewater Golf Club.

17   With Lt. Norman Tharp inspected the Douglas and Buick plants. Douglas produces 15 C-54 airplanes a month. Allies outflank Cassino.

18   Cassino, Italy falls to Allies. Strikes slow up production.

19   US House of Representatives passes GI Bill of Rights.

22   Allies advance in Italy and China.

23   Staff visit to Milwaukee area office. I gave a talk to the inspection trainee graduates.

25   US forces meet in Italy. 7,500 allied planes blast Europe.

26   I conducted the conference of our five area personnel officers.

29   Allies near Rome.

June 1   3,657,000 US troops now overseas. 5,000,000 by end of the year.

2   US planes bomb from Red bases.

5   Allies enter Rome. King Emmanuel abdicates to his son. Nazi retreat north of Rome as US 5th Army pursues.

6   Allies invade France—D-Day, 4,000 ships, 11,000 planes attack Le Havre, Rouen and Cherbourg area.

7   Major General Henry J. F. Miller demoted to lieut. colonel for revealing D-Day time at a social party in London.

8   Allies push inland in France.

9   General Eisenhower sets up HQ in France. Paratroops and planes attack. Generals Marshall and Arnold and Admiral King land in England for Allied Command conference.

10   Allies pour in troops on the 40 mile beachhead in Normandy—13 miles to Cherbourg. Air bases established.

12   Churchill, Generals Eisenhower, Marshall and Arnold visit beachhead in France.

14   Colonel Schlotzhaur, district administrative executive, inspected the Studebaker plant in South Bend.

15   Generals Jones, Wood and Hopkins held Termination and Property Disposal Conference all day. Luncheon at the University Club. US B-29's bomb Japan—first time.

June 16   US B-29's knock out steel plants in Japan. Allies advance in Normandy. Nazi use Rocket Planes.

18   All MCPD officers and their wives attended a Tea Dance at the Knickerbocker Hotel.

19   Art Lovell took my assistant Captain Siwek and me all thru the Dodge-Chicago plant—the world's largest.

21   I presented 3 medals to parents of a Swedish captain and Jewish lieutenant killed in action. A very unpleasant task. Busy on Manpower Survey Conference. US troops in Cherbourg.

22   Busy at Manpower Conference. FDR signs GI Bill.

23   US troops enter Cherbourg. Reds start drive to Berlin as allies advance in France and Italy.

26   Arrive in St. Louis, Mo. 7:30 A.M. To Melbourne Hotel for Materiel Command Personnel Conference. All district Civ. pers. officers, HQ MC staff and Colonel Clark HQ AAF, as well as a representative of the office secy. of war.

27   All conference members take boat ride on steamer on the Mississippi tonite. 102° hot!

28   All conferees went thru the plant of Anheuser-Busch brewery, the world's largest. The plant makes gliders for the air force.

30   HQ, office Secretary of War audit completed of my personnel program and we received an excellent report. We also hit 90% participation and 10% payroll reservation in War Bonds for Treasury Dept. Flag.

July 2   SUNDAY. Slept till 6:30 P.M. Took 11:05 P.M. train for Dayton, Ohio, with Lt. Col. E. A. Mattison. Before the war he was V.P. of Bank of America in SF.

3   Spent the day in a Termination of Contracts Conference.

6   Robot bombs kill 2,750 people in southern England.

7   We had a reception at the Knickerbocker Hotel Officers' Club for our commander, Colonel Salsman, who is leaving for overseas duty.

8   Allies near Caen, France and Reds nearing Poland.

10   Col. Nelson Talbott takes command of the district and gives a talk.

July 12   Busy on manpower survey and personnel freeze. Yanks take Saipan.

13   Reds 30 mi. from Prussia. Germans in terror.

14   Played golf at Evanston Golf Course with Major Olson and Lieutenant Merry.

15   Lieutenant General Knudsen to head combined materiel command and air service command.

17   US troops take St. Lo, France. Busy on manpower survey and problems.

20   Hitler injured by assassination bomb.

21   Hitler purges army clique and civil disturbance is going on in Germany. Senator Truman nominated for V.P. on Democratic ticket.

22   General Tojo's cabinet kicked out in Japan.

25   Went to South Bend with Lt. Colonel Eddy concerning the deactivation of the South Bend Area. Hitler appoints Marshal Goering as mobilization director as officer purge continues.

26   Had argument with Colonel Talbott and Lt. Colonel Mattison on manpower utilization. Captain Stevenson backed me up.

27   Worked till 9 P.M. with Colonel Mattison on estimates for readjustment personnel. Gen. Leslie McNair is killed.

30   Reds enter East Prussia.

31   At a celebration and ceremony the treasury dept. awarded Colonel Talbott, our commander, the "T" Flag for the MCPD achieving 90% participation and 10% War Bond Pay Reservation of the 5th War Loan Drive. Gen. K. B. Wolfe gave a talk. I am the District War Bond Officer. *[See part 2C, chapter VI.]*

Aug. 1   Busy all day in manpower conference to reduce personnel.

7   US troops 100 miles from Paris.

9   I am making an effort to get transferred to ASC thru my former boss and friend Colonel Wood at HQ, ASC.

10   FDR met General MacArthur and admirals in Hawaii. B-29's keep bombing Japan.

12   Busy on manpower studies and surveys.

Aug. 13	US troops about to trap 300,000 Nazi in France.
14	HQ, materiel command recommending I be assigned to NYC at eastern procurement district or western procurement district at LA due to conditions that had to be corrected there.
15	US troops land on southern coast of France and head north and meet our troops in Brittany. Hoping for transfer orders to ASC.
19	US troops enter Paris suburbs.
21	All my area civilian personnel officers here for a meeting today. All MC district supervisors here too.
23	Allies take Marseilles. Paris falls to French patriots and Rumania battles Nazi and Hungary.
25	French troops reach Paris. General DeGaulle in Paris.
27	General Eisenhower enters Paris. Bulgaria now neutral.
30	Captain Siwek and I are having trouble with Lieutenant Rubin. Must get him out.
31	Relieved today as district civilian personnel officer and promoted to asst. admin. executive to the district supervisor [commander]. Today the AAF Air Service Command and the Materiel Command are combined into the AAF Air Technical Services Command.
Sept. 1	I took Captain Siwek and M. Levin to our Milwaukee area office to discuss personnel problems and the reduction in personnel at the Allis-Chalmers plant.
2	Our 5th wedding anniversary. Allies enter Belgium and German borders.
4	Allies in Antwerp, Belgium and Holland.
5	Demobilization plans to be announced tomorrow.
7	Received my orders at last! The office had a dinner for one of my clerks, Marge Dalton, who is getting married, and for me at the Normandie Hotel. About 25 people there. They gave me a pipe.
11	Reported to Col. W. W. Wood, my former boss at HQ, AAF Material Command, Wright Field. It is now HQ Air Technical Service Command, they merged. He assigned me to the military personnel division for 30 days orientation on command policies, etc.

Sept. 18   Received letter from Col. Nelson Talbott, my previous boss in Chicago, about the good cooperation and work he had received from me while in the Chicago Office.

21   Had dinner with Col. Richard Gimble. In private life he is part owner of the Gimble Department Store Chain.

26   Allies have a hard fight at Arulie and the Moselle River area.

30   Allies slowed at Siegfried Line. Reds invade Yugoslavia.

Oct. 2   I received a letter of commendation from Gen. Lucius Beau, Col. Nelson Talbott, my old boss in Chicago, and Lt. Col. Paul Bell, chief of military personnel, HQ, ATSC for my outstanding performance of duty in my duty assignment in Chicago.

9   Allies advance thru Aachen in Germany.

16   Lt. Colonel White wants me in his civilian personnel division, HQ, ATSC.

17   B-29's blast Formosa again.

18   US and British planes blast Cologne, Germany.

19   US troops invade Philippines.

23   Got Lieutenant Bolen out of bed to dispensary this P.M.

25   Talked to General Beau about Lt. Colonel White and personnel problems in the HQ and field.

27   Attended AAF Procurement District Personnel Conference.

28   US blasts most of Jap Navy out of Philippine waters.

30   US Navy knocks out 58 Jap ships in Philippine sea battle. Nazi retreat in Holland. Dewey campaigns for president.

Nov. 1   US B-29's blast Tokyo. Gen. Joe Stillwell recalled from CBI at request of Chiang Kai-Shek.

2   US takes over Leyte Island.

3   Conference on reduction in force all day.

7   Major Jim Gaylord and I arrived in LA via TWA 6 P.M. Saw Eddie Bracken, the movie actor, at the airport.

8   Went to Cocoanut Grove last nite, staying at the Ambassador Hotel. FDR elected 4th time. Went to W.P. District HQ. Visited Town and Country Market.

Nov. 9   Arrived at HQ, San Bernardino ATSC for ATSC Personnel Officers' Conference. Formal dinner dance at Officers' Club. Dorothy Lamour and Kenny Baker put on show.

11   Left San Bernardino on the Santa Fe "Super Chief" train for Dayton.

15   US troops advance in Metz, France area.

17   Six US armies advance toward Rhine River in Germany.

20   Allies take Metz. US loses 10 ships in S.W. Pacific.

21   U.S. B-29's continue to bomb Japan.

22   Received my new assignment. I am to be asst. chief Personnel and Training Division, HQ, Pacific Overseas Air Technical Service Command, Oakland, Calif., under Colonel Leslie Ross.

28   En route to California. At Vandalia, Ill. tonite.

29   At Springfield, Mo. tonite.

30   Had to stop and get radiator unfrozen and install a water pump at Oklahoma City, Ok. tonite.

Dec. 1   At Tucumcari, N.M. tonite 6 P.M.

2   At Gallup, N.M. Hotel El Rancho. Lots of Indians here.

3   At Needles, Calif. tonite. Drove thru Painted Desert, Petrified Forest and snow in mountains.

4   Drove thru desert to San Bernardino, Pasadena to LA and Hollywood, Mayo Motel.

5   Shopped at the "Miracle Mile" and Town and Country Market and to Santa Monica. Dinner at the "Tropics."

6   Left LA Drove to Santa Barbara, Ventura and San Luis Obispo. Had a tire blow out.

7   Arrived in SF and Oakland. Finally got a place to stay in Berkeley at Univ. of Calif. campus area.

8   Reported to HQ, Pacific Overseas Air Technical Service Command, 1950 Broadway, Oakland, California. Assigned as administrative assistant and control officer, Personnel and Base Services Division.

CHAPTER IV

HQ POATSC was located in a large downtown office building. The command was responsible for receiving, from production sources, aircraft and aircraft equipment and supplies; maintaining necessary stocks upon which the using units in the Pacific Theatre of Operations could draw; providing for overhaul and heavy repair work and salvages damaged or excess material returned from Pacific bases. The command scheduled equipment and supplies which were required by Pacific Air Force units so that they could be ordered, delivered and stocked. The command carried out these functions through the direction and operation of three Intransit Depots located at Tacoma, Wash., Oakland and Long Beach, Calif. These were water ports for shipments overseas and receipt of aircraft, equipment and supplies from overseas installations. The August 1945 personnel strength of the command totaled 6,687, comprising the following categories:

Civilian civil service employees	*3,168*
Military	*1,689*
Manual service labor (cargo)	*1,445*
Manual service (aircraft)	*385*

Dec. 9   I have 7 WACS (Women's Army Corps members) and two civilian female employees, all new—to be trained.

13   Tokyo bombed again.

Dec. 15 We moved into a room in a private home $50.00 mo. Lupe Valez, movie actress, killed herself.

16 Gen. MacArthur splits Philippine defenses. US 9th Army in Germany.

18 Nazi launch tremendous counter-drive in Belgium and Luxembourg area. 21 mile drive. B-29's blast Japan.

20 Nazi drive on and kill US prisoners.

28 Yanks stop Nazi drive.

30 Some girl tried to show me SF this P.M. when I went over to get tickets for the East-West game New Year's day at Kesar Stadium.

1945

Jan. 1 We went to Shriners East-West Football game at Kesar Stadium. SF South Pacific train wreck kills 48, injures 80.

3 Nazis push 7th US Army back.

4 Japs lose 95 ships.

5 British Field Marshal Montgomery in command of 1st and 9th US Armies.

8 General MacArthur invades Luzon, Philippines.

10 General MacArthur lands 100,000 troops in Luzon.

11 Allies push bulge out in Belgium. Capt. Morton Goldberg is my new assistant. A National Service Law is requested by FDR.

12 Gen. William Farthing assumed command at a meeting of all officers. He was commanding officer of Hickam Field when Japs attacked Pearl Harbor.

13 US Navy defeats Japs and sink 84 ships in India-Burma-Philippines area. Major Richard Borg who shot down 40 planes in the Pacific area gets Congressional Medal of Honor. Reds advance in Poland.

17 Reds take Warsaw, Poland.

18 Reds enter German Silesia and Prussia. Half of our division is moving to new building at Alameda.

19 Elliott Roosevelt's dog gets "A" priority in plane shipment.

Jan. 20   FDR sworn in for 4th time.

22   Reds 135 miles from Berlin. MacArthur 60 miles from Manila.

23   Worked till midnite on organization of our division.

24   Worked till 8:30 P.M. Gen. H. H. Arnold says all AAF personnel will no doubt see overseas service.

25   US troop ship sunk with losses of 746 lives. Colonel Ross gave me "Superior" on Efficiency Report. Our Division has about 580 personnel assigned. Worked till 7 P.M.

26   Reds 90 miles from Berlin. Japs flee Manila area.

28   We toured SF.

30   Don't expect any more promotions due to overstrength and reduced allotments.

31   Working days and nights on reorganization and expansion. Colonel Ross leans heavily on me for administration and control.

Feb. 1   Gen. MacArthur releases 513 US troops held as prisoners by Japs.

4   MacArthur's 1st Cavalry enters Manila.

6   Japs burn Manila. Working late daily.

7   US 37th Division mops up Manila.

8   We have 5 officers and 532 personnel in our Division.

9   Captain Goldberg and I worked till 1:15 A.M. tonite on strength and allotment problem.

11   SUNDAY. Conference at office 10:30–1:30 P.M.

12   FDR, Churchill and Stalin hold 8 day conference in Crimea and set rules for defeat of Germany and occupation of it. Elliott Roosevelt made brig. gen.

13   SF to be site of United Nations Peace Conference April 26.

15   We went to "Top of the Mark" Hopkins Hotel in SF. View of the whole Bay area. Dinner in Chinatown at the Cathay House.

16   Bataan captured by US troops. 1,500 planes blast Tokyo.

17   US troops take Corregidor from Japs. US B-29's bomb Tokyo.

Feb. 21	25 Jap ships sunk. 3,650 casualties on Iwo Jima in first 48 hours.
23	Turkey to declare war on Axis. Our manpower crisis is getting worse.
25	Toured SF.
26	200 B-29's blast Tokyo.
27	1,000 US carrier planes and 200 B-29's bomb Tokyo. Allies approach Cologne and Nazi are retreating on western front. I turned our control section over to Captain Austin Gallup.
29	FDR talks to Congress about World Peace Parley in SF in April. He outlines plans developed at Yalta Conference on German and Jap surrender. Yanks in Cologne on Rhine.
March 3	Nazi blow up bridges over Rhine and retreat in disorder. Lt. General Harmon lost in Pacific plane crash.
4	Yanks 3 mi. from Cologne. All but 500 yards of Iwo Jima taken.
6	Captain Goldberg and I depart for LA and Long Beach Depots on three day inspection trip. Bought a battle jacket at P.O.E.
9	300 B-29's bomb Tokyo.
10	Arrived in Oakland 9 A.M. Our office moved to new administration bldg. in Alameda. *[See part 3, chapter VI.]*
13	US B-29's bomb Osaka, Japan.
15	Allies advance closer to Berlin. Tokyo bombed again.
16	300 B-29's blast Kobe, Japan. US troops take Coblenz, Germany.
19	US B-29's and carrier based planes blast Japan.
20	Allies advance in Germany and Nazi collapse in Saar region.
22	100,000 Nazi troops taken in Saar. Reds push thru Silesia.
23	Ruhr Valley and Rhine area pounded by allied planes. Tokyo preparing for island defense.
25	Nazi routed by 6 allied armies converging on Berlin.
27	Argentina declares war on Axis—a little late!

March 28	Nazi cry for mercy as we get closer to Berlin.
31	General Eisenhower says Nazi armies are beaten. US troops take Okinawa.
April 2	Nazi retreat in Holland. Fred Vinson takes over as director of war mobilization.
6	Reds in Vienna.
9	British troops near Bremen.
12	President Roosevelt dies at 3:35 P.M. I was playing golf at Alameda Municipal Golf Course when flag was lowered at half mast. World mourns. Radio programs cancelled.
13	Truman calls cabinet meeting.
14	FDR returned to White House from Georgia. Elliott was his only son there. US 9th Army nearing Berlin. Bombs strike Japanese Imperial Palace.
15	FDR funeral service at Hyde Park, NY home.
18	General Patton's 3rd Army enters Czechoslovakia. Ernie Pyle killed by Japs near Okinawa.
19	Yanks take Leipzig. Played golf at Clarmont C.C.
23	Reds in Berlin.
24	Saw some of the Arabian delegation members at the Clarmont Hotel in Berkeley. They are attending the UN Conference. Their goats take up one whole floor!
25	United Nations Security Conference in SF. The hope of a world peace organization may be realized but I wonder if it will succeed—human nature being what it is.
26	British troops take Bremen. Reds in Berlin.
27	Reds and Yanks join forces on Elbe River near Leipzig.
29	Mussolini shot and hanged in Milan, Italy by patriots. Three quarters of Berlin in Red hands.
30	Had lunch with American Trust Co. officials at Alameda facility. Pictures taken. A plot to kill MacArthur on May Day was uncovered.
May 1	Berlin reports that Hitler was killed in his command post in the chancellery. Admiral Doenitz announces he has been appointed his successor.

May 2   President Truman says Hitler is dead. German Field Marshal Von Runstedt is captured. All Nazi armies in Italy surrender to General Alexander. Reds control Berlin.

3   Pierre Laval, premier of France, in Spanish jail to be handed over to United Nations. *[Later executed for treason.]* Nazi retreat in Norway and Denmark as British take Hamburg.

6   German Army surrenders to General Eisenhower 5:41 P.M.

8   V-E Day Victory half won! Announced by President Truman and General Eisenhower. 5 years, 8 months of war ends in Europe.

9   Nazi Field Marshals Goering and Kesselring captured. Field Marshal Keitel signs ratification surrender in Berlin to Russian General Zhukov.

10   US Army discharge plan announced. 1,500,000 troops to be released in a year. Played golf at Clarmont C.C.

14   500 B-29's blast Nagoya, Japan, aircraft plants.

16   Naka, Okinawa, captured. 500 more US B-29's blast Nagoya aircraft plants. Played golf at Clarmont C.C.

20   Inspected Kaiser Richmond shipyards and saw Liberty ships being made.

21   General Hodges' 1st US Army on way to Pacific.

23   Assigned as chief of civilian personnel, replacing Major Len Larson.

24   Nazi Himmler, the hangman of Germany, kills himself with poison on capture. Capt. E. J. Bennett, one of my assistants, and I made an inspection trip to Alcatraz Prison in SF Bay. Warden Johnson had us for lunch in his lovely dining room with a beautiful view of the SF Bay and bridges and mountains. 12 acres of the "Rock." Saw Al Karpis, Machine Gun Kelly, the Bird Man of Alcatraz and a German saboteur prisoner. Average sentence of the 250 toughest prisoners in the US was 32 years. *[See part 3A, chapter VI.]*

25   500 US B-29's bomb Tokyo again. 500,000 autos approved for manufacture.

26   Visited housing project in Berkeley and Albany. Tokyo devastated. General Doolittle's 8th Air Force goes to the Pacific.

May 28   Shipyards lay off 21,000 during April in the Bay area.

29   51 sq. miles of Tokyo destroyed by B-29's. Yokohama now on fire.

30   Labor crisis here in manpower shortage and turnover.

31   Manpower problems critical. Contacted War Manpower Commission representative on priority urgency committee in SF to start inter-regional recruiting.

June 1   Called Colonel Berg, HQ, ATSC, on manpower problems. Played golf at Clarmont C.C. Someone broke into my car last nite.

2   Gen. Bennett Meyers in trouble with the Senate Truman Committee. Had several sets of books kept on aircraft production and scheduling. He was removed and retired.

3   Officers and their families picnic and boat ride from Camp Knight to Marin County by Treasure Island, Angle Island and Sausalito. A wonderful all day outing.

4   Need more employees for our Returned Cargo Distribution Program.

7   Made presentation to our commander, General Farthing, and Colonel Burns on our critical manpower problems. He commended me and wants me to present it at a HQ staff meeting Saturday.

8   Big fire at Oakland Army Base. Over 420 ships are in the Bay awaiting repairs. Manpower problems desperate.

9   Made presentation before General Farthing and his staff about manpower problems. The general complimented me and backed me 100% on the program.

12   Attended a meeting of the Congress for International Organization at the SF Opera House. The French Foreign Minister Binaut talked about the Security Council. 50 nations were represented.

14   US troops push 10,000 Japs to the sea in Okinawa. India is offered Home Rule by the British. Nazi Foreign Minister Von Ribbentrop captured by British in Hamburg. Going to get rid of Captain Brown and Mrs. Newman in Employment and Placement Branch.

19   Working with the War Manpower Commission and Civil Service Commission on the recruitment problem.

June 20	Major General Bennett Meyers reduced in rank to a Lt. Colonel and retired by President Truman for corrupt arrangements in contracts with aircraft companies.
26	President Truman addressed the SF UN conference.
27	World Charter of United Nations signed at SF meeting. Island of Luzon in Philippines is liberated.
28	Played golf at Clarmont C.C.
29	US B-29's blast Japan's home islands.
30	Major Gen. Hugh Knerr is new commander of the Air Technical Service Command.
July 3	Four big Japanese industrial cities blasted by 450-500 B-29's.
4	Tired of all this—wish I were out on a ranch in the mountain with some peace and quiet around me!
7	On leave. We are at the Ambassador Hotel in LA.
8	On leave. We are at the US Grant Hotel in San Diego. Visited Ti Juana, Mexico.
10	Visited Park Zoo in San Diego. At Treymore Hotel in LA.
12	We are having housing problems for employees of our command.
13	Attended Conference of Bay Area Personnel Officers of the Civil Service Commission, Air Force, Army and Navy.
14	I had Captain Brown reassigned out of my organization.
16	My wife wants me to get out of the Army.
17	Japan blasted by US planes daily. Visited Mills College to see about housing for some of our employees.
18	Housing and transportation problems are severe for female employees transferred here from East Coast.
19	I took a ride across The Alameda Estuary with a maritime officer. Arranging for a ferry for our personnel to use. Played golf.
20	Worked till 8 P.M. on the Reclassification and Salaries Project covering graded employees. Japan bombed daily.
21	A motor ferry across the Estuary at Alameda being worked out with the Navy. Lt. Col. Burton Fitts of LA, and former lt. governor of California, and LA district attorney, are working on the project.

July 22 Officers' Club Picnic at Redwood Canyon. Grand day in the beautiful Redwoods.

23 A man and his six year old daughter die in jump from Golden Gate Bridge.

24 Conference of Truman, Stalin and Churchill in progress.

25 Went to party at Bob Gardreys. Got sick. Davidson brought us home—Janie told me this would happen! She's smarter than I am.

26 Attlee replaces Churchill as prime minister of Great Britain.

27 I am on list of 185 officers up for overseas consideration.

28 A B-25 aircraft crashes into Empire State Bldg. in NYC. 18 killed.

31 Attended Civilian Personnel Officers' Conference. Gen. Elliott Roosevelt asks for relief from active duty—has trouble with some of his borrowings. Japs lose 1,541 ships and 1,300 planes in June. 800 B-29's hit Japs with 6,000 tons of fire.

Aug. 1 Air Force Day at Alameda. Big review and ceremony.

3 Capt. Ed Bennet is being reassigned to Control Section to replace Major Larson. Ed hasn't been able to get along with people.

4 General MacArthur takes command of all Army forces for invasion of Japan. 12 more Jap cities on death list for bombing to bits.

5 SUNDAY. All employees of my office enjoyed a picnic at March Creek at the foot of Mt. Diablo, about 3,500 feet elevation.

6 US aircraft drops Atomic bomb on Japan. Most terrific of all power yet devised. Major Bong, Pacific Theatre's Ace fighter pilot, killed in crash.

7 I took Southern Pacific Overland Ltd. Train for Chicago 8 P.M. en route to AAF Staff School, Applied Personnel Management Course. AAF Center, Orlando, Fla.

8 President Truman announces Russia declares war on Japan tomorrow 9 Aug. Atomic bomb completely destroys 60% of Hiroshima. More to be dropped.

Aug. 9   Traveled thru Cheyenne, Wyo. this A.M. Freight cars derailment causes 2 1/2 hr. delay in getting to Omaha, Neb. tonite.

10   Japan offers to surrender if Hiroshima is spared. Arr. in Chicago, 11 A.M.

11   Allies O.K. Jap peace if Emperor Hirohito takes orders from allied supreme commander. Went thru Nashville, Atlanta this P.M.

12   On train last nite to Jacksonville a medical officer, a major, took pills and died in the berth next to mine. They stopped the train and took him out thru a window. Quite an experience! Arrived in Orlando, Fla. 2 P.M. Reported in.

14   President Truman announced acceptance of surrender terms by Japan at 7 P.M. First day of my course of study at the school. We are restricted to the base. Went swimming and sail boating on the lake on the base in Orlando.

15   School dismissed. Review and ceremonies at 9:55 A.M. Holiday today and tomorrow. Gas rationing discontinued.

17   Very interesting course of study. Officers talking about getting out of service.

18   Visited my parents in St. Petersburg.

24   Graduated from AAF Applied Personnel Management Course.

25   Visited my parents. 6" of rainfall.

27   Left 9:15 P.M. from Jacksonville for Chicago.

28   US advance troops land in Tokyo.

29   President Truman announces facts about Pearl Harbor.

30   US troops land in Yokohama.

31   On the train's observation car we went over Great Salt Lake in Utah.

Sept. 1   Arrived back in Oakland 10 A.M. Our command back on a 40 hour week.

2   V-J Day declared by President Truman. The war is now over! This is our 6th wedding anniversary!

Sept. 3   Labor Day. I took Major Paul Just, Capt., and Mrs. Gallop up to Colonel Leslie Ross's home for his birthday party. He is our boss. General Farthing, our commander, his wife and others were there.

4   Age for release of soldiers and sailors reduced to age 35. Exodus now for troops to get out. We have let 425 civilian employees go.

5   General Wainwright nominated for fourth star. Employees rushing to leave the command—same with the GI's.

6   Conference with deputy commander, Colonel Porter. Points for release from duty announced. 100 required for field grade officers for discharge. President Truman announces 21 points for Peace Time Program. General MacArthur in Tokyo.

8   Big Victory Parade in SF for General Wainwright and returning veterans.

9   Visit and picnic at beautiful Hearst Ranch.

10   Took my wife to the Red Cross. She went to SF on a tug boat out in the Bay and in the ocean by the Golden Gate Bridge to welcome and meet incoming Pacific veterans on transport ships.

11   General Tojo, Japan's military leader, shot himself.

12   Busy reassigning employees and cutting down overtime. Jap war criminals being arrested. Former war minister killed himself.

13   2,000,000 veterans to be released by Christmas.

15   Played golf with Major Johnny Wall at Tilden Park in Berkeley Hills.

16   Strikes and unemployment prevalent.

17   General MacArthur to use less than 200,000 troops in Japan. Strikes tie up 215,000 CIO workers.

18   Visited Gumps' Jewelry store in SF. Saw $45,000 Jade necklace. Went thru Treasure Island. Sec'y of War Stimson resigns.

19   Accompanied Colonel Ross to dinner given by Oakland Area Community War Chest Committee. Admiral Gaffney there. B-29's from Japan land in Chicago.

Sept. 20   Congress hot on demobilization.

21   About 40 of our officers requested consideration for Regular Army Commissions. My wife wants me out of service.

24   Busy with our commander, General Farthing, and Colonel Porter concerning the Dade Bros. Contract employees. The General called HQ, ATSC for approval for higher pay rates.

25   Conference with Colonel Hassen and Major Loupos all A.M. on job analysis of employees due to reorganizations.

26   We took a boat ride on a 42' Army boat around Alcatraz and Angel Islands and Richmond. We saw a ship made of concrete. Emperor Hirohito sees General MacArthur.

27   Colonel Ohmer, Deputy Commander, sent me a hot memo about personnel problems. We had a conference about supply div. jobs.

28   Busy on conversion of military to civilian jobs and classification surveys of positions.

29   Visited beautiful Yosemite Nat'l Park. Climbed to Glacier Point 7,300 ft. Gorgeous view of valley. Bears too.

30   We went thru Maraposa Grove of Trees. Saw 3,800 year old "Grizzley Giant" tree—30 ft. thru. Drove thru "Wawena" tree. Park is the size of Rhode Island.

Oct. 1   Colonel Porter and I talked to Dade Bros. contract employees. Difficult to get people to replace military personnel.

2   Chester Quick, one of my classification analysts, and I left on the Southern Pacific R.R. "Cascade" train for Tacoma, Wash. General Eisenhower fires General Patton.

4   Went to Baker Dock, then to Auburn office.

5   At Winthrop Hotel. At 4:15 A.M. fire broke out on the 4th floor in a room directly under our room at the hotel. A veteran was burned and taken to the hospital. $10,000 in damage. *[See part 4 (10), chapter VI.]* We took a boat ride across Puget Sound, Seattle and Bremerton.

Oct. 8 Problems with Colonel Porter concerning his desire for higher pay for Dade Bros. Contract employees. I took Bob Hipp, from HQ, AAF Directorate of Civilian Personnel, with me to see Colonel Ohmer, deputy commander, and Colonel Ross about this pay problem for Dade Bros. Contract employees.

9 We went thru the big USS *Ticonderoga* aircraft carrier and the baby flat top USS *Anzio*, both veterans of the Jap war. *[See part 3B, chapter VI.]*

13 Duty officer in the general's office Saturday.

15 I was promoted to chief, personnel and training division of our command. Admiral "Bull" Halsey's 3rd US Fleet in SF Bay. *[See part 3B, chapter VI.]*

19 General Farthing doesn't know what his workload is to be and is having trouble getting funds and allotments.

22 Our officer force moving into administration bldg. at Alameda today. I move in with Colonel Ross.

23 I was appointed chairman, Personnel Management Committee of the Federal Personnel Council of SF.

24 Found out Colonel Ross rated me No. 1 of 7 officers in my grade under him and Gen. W. E. Farthing rated me No. 12 of the 100 officers known to him in recommending me for the Regular Army.

26 CIO-GMC strike about to tie up over 300,000 workers.

27 Navy Day. We took a motor launch trip to SF and saw the battleships *Alabama* and *South Dakota* of Admiral "Bull" Halsey's 3rd Fleet and his flagship *Wisconsin*, as well as the big carriers *Yorktown* and *Bon Homme Richard*, and the cruiser *Oakland*, and three submarines. *[See part 3B, chapter VI.]*

30 President Truman talks on radio about wages and prices. Strikes throughout the nation. Shoe rationing ends.

Nov. 3 General Doolittle here at his Alameda home for celebration. Civil war rages in China.

5 Busy with Colonel Ross, Colonel Ohmer and General Farthing working on Manning Tables.

13 Took a tour thru the USS *Tulage*, an aircraft carrier that was in both the Atlantic and Pacific areas.

Nov. 17   Visited Richmond, Telegraph Hill and Golden Gate Bridge.

20   Trial of Nazi Field Marshal Goering and others starts today.

21   Comedian Robert Benchley and Gen. Alexander Patch died.

26   Auto strikes continue.

28   General Farthing said Intransit Depot #2 Tacoma, Wash. to be inactivated by 1 April.

29   59,000 members of the armed forces being released daily. 3,500,000 to date.

Dec. 2   An earthquake shook the church we attended this morning.

9   Jap General Yamashito convicted.

10   General Patton's back was injured in auto accident in Germany.

11   Strikes continue to tie up industries. All field grade promotions are frozen.

15   Gen. George Marshall named ambassador to China.

18   50,000 GI's in Bay area clog transportation lines.

19   My promotion to lieutenant colonel held up due to 60 day freeze on promotions.

21   Gen. George Patton dies in Heidelberg from accident. 338,000 vets out of work.

25   First Christmas of peace in 5 years.

31   New Year's Eve party at Major Nick Loupos' home. A number of officers and wives there.

1946

Jan. 1   We attended the 21st Annual East-West Shrine Football Game at Kesar Stadium in SF. Governor Warren sat just several feet behind us. We split the 50 yd. marker in half!

2   Major Jim Gaylord at Wright Field called me and wanted me to get out and go to work for the Penna. Central Airlines.

Jan. 3   President Truman talks on the radio to the nation on the strike situation and reconversion program.

6   US troops in Manila protest delays in coming home, slow demobilization and lack of replacements.

7   10,000 GI's in Manila jeer Lt. Gen. W. D. Styer and demonstrate to "come home."

9   GI's demonstrate in Manila, Germany and Japan.

10   Our deputy commander, Colonel Ohmer, says Col. W. W. Wood at HQ, ATSC, Wright Field, Ohio wants me to return there and take a job he has for me.

11   GMC-CIO and Big Steel fighting over bargaining wages.

14   Worldwide social and economic revolution. Result of chaotic atomic era of uncertainty.

15   300,000 electrical workers, 200,000 meat packers are going on strike with GMC auto workers. General Eisenhower speaks to Congress on demobilization.

18   General Eisenhower talks to overseas GI's on radio about demobilization.

20   Over 1,500,000 workers on strike. Nation in bad shape.

25   Lt. General Twining, Commander of ATSC, Maj. General Chidlaw and General Gerry here on inspection trip.

29   Radio-radio controlled missiles make it about possible to bomb any place on earth.

31   My commander, General Farthing, sent a letter to HQ, ATSC, recommending that I be awarded the Army Commendation Medal for my outstanding work here.

Feb. 4   My father passed away in St. Petersburg, Fla.

9   1,445,000 people on strike in US.

14   St. Valentine's Day. Received promotion to lieutenant colonel. Received my second Award of the Army Commendation Medal for Outstanding Performance of Duty. Citation signed by commander, AAF Materiel Command.

16   Departed HQ, POATSC for new job at HQ, ATSC, Wright Field, Ohio under Colonel W. W. Wood.

17   Stayed with friends in LA tonite.

19   Stayed at Tucson, Ariz. Army Base.

Feb. 20	Stayed at El Paso, Texas. Visited Juarez, Mexico.
21	Stayed at Sonara, Texas.
22	Stayed at Houston, Texas.
23	Stayed at Baton Rouge, La.
24	Stayed at New Orleans, La. At Mobile, Ala. tonite.
25	Thru Tallahassee to Perry, Fla. tonite.
26	Arrived at my mother's home in St. Petersburg, Fla.

March 4	Went to funeral home to get my father's ashes to take to Harrisonburg, Va. for burial.
5	Left St. Petersburg, Fla. and stayed at Waycross, Ga. tonite.
6	To Greenville, S.C. and Spartanburg, S.C. and visited friends.
7	To Kings Mountain, N.C. to visit Dr. Jake Mauney, my old fraternity brother, and then on to Bassett, Va.
8	Arrived at Kavanaugh Hotel, Harrisonburg, Va.
10	Attended funeral services with Masonic rites for the burial of my father, Wilmer E. Swank, at Woodbine Cemetery, Harrisonburg, Va.
12	This would have been my father's 80th birthday. Staying with friends in Fairfax, Va. tonite.
14	Visited the Pentagon. The chief of engineers offered me a position. Also, Capt. Bill Doddridge in General Bradley's office in the Veterans Administration said he had a job for me.
18	Drove to Columbus, Ohio, my wife's family home. Finished a 5,235 mile trip from California.
19	Visited Col. W. W. Wood at Wright Field, Ohio. I am to report for work the 26th.

CHAPTER V

This command was created in August 1943 when the AAF Materiel Command [chapter II] and the AAF Service Command were combined.

The latter organization was responsible for distribution and supply to AAF units of equipment and supplies; maintenance and repair of aircraft; training of service, supply and maintenance units for assignment overseas. In addition to large military components, approximately 183,000 civilian employees were employed in the ASC depots throughout the country in maintenance, repair and supply of aircraft, engines and radios. Over 35,000 employees were assigned to procurement activities of the Materiel Command.

During this early post-war period the AAF was in the throes of major adjustments and realignments in operations and functions to establish a down-sized peace time organizational structure.

Reductions in force, base closings, production contract readjustments and consolidation and changes in strategic, tactical and logistical organizations were required.

The war had demonstrated the overwhelming impact and importance of air power.

No war could be won without air superiority and no war could be lost with it.

Recognition by Congress of the need for a separate Department of the Air Force was now at hand.

In September 1947, Congress established a separate US Air Force and the Department of the Air Force under a new Department of Defense.

March 26	Reported for duty. I am Col. Ralph Penland's assistant, managing the Wright-Patterson AFB, Ohio, civilian personnel office which has 780 employees. This office services over 25,000 employees on the base.
28	Busy, tired—in a puzzled state of mind as to job, outside opportunities, future, housing problems and various other things. Guess all will be o.k.—but often wonder.
April 4	My emotions are restless. Guess it takes time to settle down.
18	Received a Distinguished Service Citation signed by the Secretary of the Treasury Fred M. Vinson, for the outstanding work I did on the War Savings Bond Program while on duty at the AAF Midcentral Procurement District in Chicago, Ill. in 1943-44. *[See part 2c, chapter VI.]*
23	Mussolini's body stolen from grave in Milan, Italy.
26	Met and talked with Arthur Fleming, US Civil Service Commissioner.
May 3	Convicts riot at Alcatraz Prison and kill the deputy warden who escorted us thru the prison last year. *[See part 3A, chapter VI.]*
6	President Truman asks for 1,070,000 man Army and seven billion dollars.
21	US to take over the coal mines tomorrow.
28	Colonel Penland to be in the hospital for some time. It puts a big workload on me.
June 4	Left for NYC on personnel business.
5	Arr. 9 A.M. To AAF Procurement Field Office, 67 Broad St. New Yorker Hotel had no rooms available so they put me up in the men's lounge!

This concludes the major aspects of the wartime diary. Chapter VI amplifies many of the key entries in the diary and related war memorabilia.

CHAPTER VI

WARTIME MEMOIRS AND COLLECTIBLES
PART 1.
WRIGHT FIELD, OHIO

Wright Field, Dayton, Ohio. Home of the Materiel Division, US Army Air Corps
Courtesy WFPL

Wright Field, Dayton, Ohio. Apron of flying field and hangars in foreground.
Courtesy WFPL

A. Captain Elliott Roosevelt [later brigadier general]

Captain Elliott Roosevelt, son of President Franklin D. Roosevelt, reported to my office for active duty at Wright Field at 4 P.M. on 9 October 1940. We had received many cards and letters addressed to him which were in my care. When we sat there talking I told him I had this correspondence and that many of the letters and cards were of a critical and vulgar nature. He said to just throw them away. Some were addressed to our commander. He was told that he would be assigned to the production engineering section and how it fitted into our activities. It was late in the afternoon when our conversation drew to a close. I told him I would take him to the hospital at adjoining Patterson Field the next morning for his physical examination.

    There was a great outpouring of resentment and ridicule by many people and the news media throughout the country about his appointment as a captain in the Army. Before destroying the correspondence I jotted down the contents of several of the items sent to him. Here they are:

Letter— Lieut. H. H. Arnold. A.C. *[Commander Army Air Forces]*

c/o Brig. Gen. Elliott Roosevelt

Wright Field, Ohio

Card—"Captain" Elliott Roosevelt

"Buck Private," Dayton, Ohio

HA HA HAW

You at last picked a soft place or was it picked for you. Patriotic me eye. Daddy of 4 boys to be shot at.

Card—Living up to family traditions, getting yourself a nice soft job just like Pappy had in the last war.

I hope nobody shoots off a cap pistol near you, it would scare the hell out of you.

Yours for promotion to Major soon.

Veteran of AEF

Card—Hurray! Am glad your propaganda peddling is off the air, you uncircumcised KIKE.

Below is a card and Western Union message that was addressed to the commanding officer, Wright Field, Ohio:

"Captain" E. Roosevelt

Protests Continue On Elliott Roosevelt

I am just as ignorant, incompetent and inexperienced in aviation as Elliot Roosevelt so send me a captain's commission too. Or do the Roosevelt family become "experts" by a stroke of the pen? H. Crowe 243 W. 4th St. N.Y.C.

CLASS OF SERVICE

This is a full-rate Telegram or Cablegram unless its deferred character is indicated by a suitable symbol above or preceding the address.

BY DIRECT WIRE FROM

WESTERN UNION

R. B. WHITE
PRESIDENT

NEWCOMB CARLTON
CHAIRMAN OF THE BOARD

J. C. WILLEVER
FIRST VICE-PRESIDENT

1223

SYMBOLS

DL=Day Letter

NL=Night Letter

LC=Deferred Cable

NLT=Cable Night Letter

Ship Radiogram

TIME at point of destination

The filing time shown in the date line on full-rate telegrams and day letters, and the time of receipt at destination as shown on all messages, is STANDARD TIME.

DA70 50 DL 3 EXTRA XC=MTHOPE WVIR OCT 15 240P

BRIG GENERAL O P ECHOLS=WRIGHT FIELD=

OBSERVING REPORT ELLIOT ROOSEVELT'S RESIGNATION UNSATISFACTORY

TO YOU BECAUSE HE IS NEEDED AS LAISON OFFICER. WISH TO

PREVENT EMBARRASMENT TO AIR CORPS AND THREATENED EMPTY POST

BY OFFERING OUR SERVICES AS CAPTAINS IN YOUR SERVICE. NOT

INTERESTED MINOR POSTS LOCAL ARRANGEMENTS FOR CONSCRIPTION

TO FILL THE RANKS=

HAROLD BRUTE LAMBERT WILLIAM L THRASHER.

346P

The following are newspaper articles and cartoons:

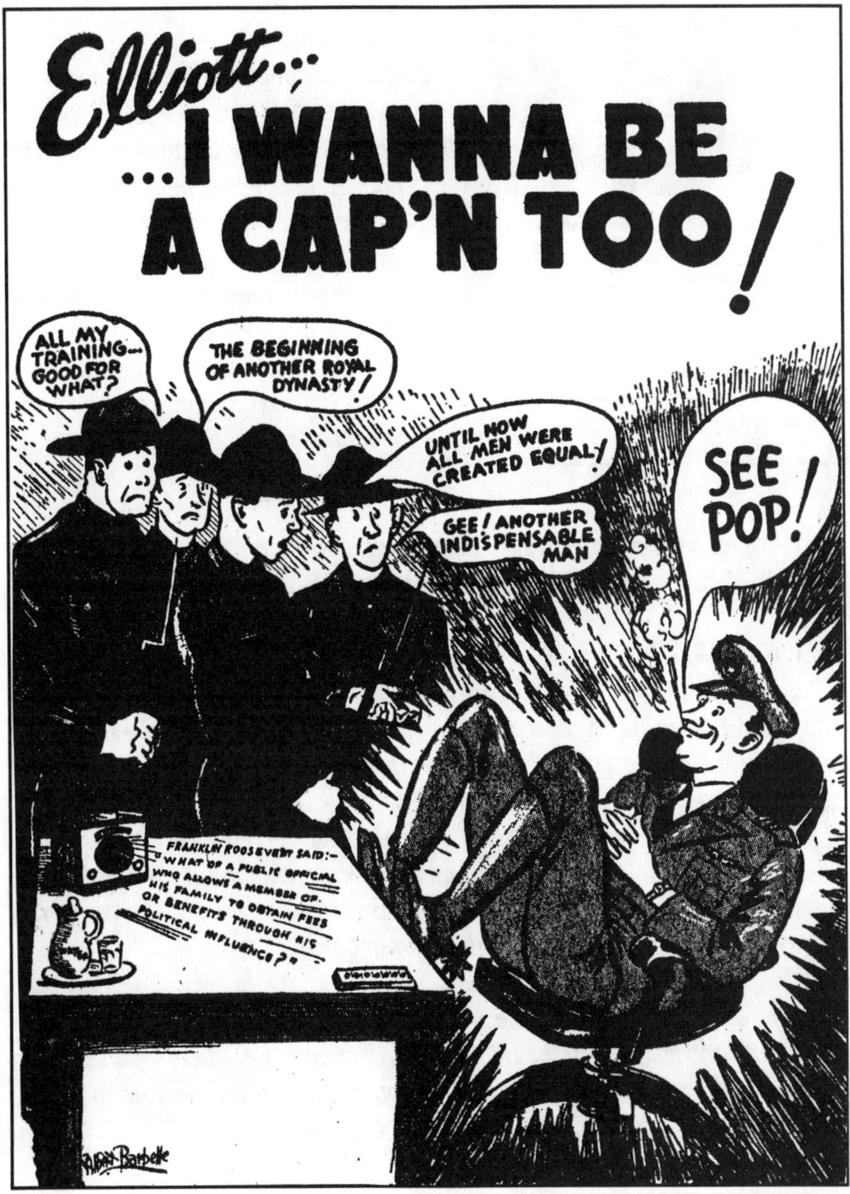

Shortly after Elliott Roosevelt, second son of the President, was accepted as a captain in the Army Air Corps, buttons of protest, like that above, made their appearance in several large United States cities. Their wearers want to be captains, too, like Captain Roosevelt, who's pictured on the button.

Captain Roosevelt Issue Blasted by Republicans

By Fred Perkins
Citizen Washington Correspondent
WASHINGTON, Oct. 7.—Republicans in Congress have begun hopping on the Captain Elliott Roosevelt issue as if it might be a vital factor in the presidential campaign.

They say they see a powerful human issue in letters and telegrams from constituents asking why they, or their sons, can't get Army commissions if the President's son can get one.

Developments in the controversy include:

1: Copies of a popular song, "Elliott, I Wanna Be a Cap'n, Too," sent from Nashville, Tenn., by the southern conference of No-Third-Term Democrats.

ELLIOTT BUTTONS

2: Receipt in Washington of the first of the Elliott Roosevelt buttons, already being worn in Chicago and New York. They look something like presidential campaign buttons and carry a portrait of young Mr. Roosevelt, with the appeal, "Elliott, I Want to Be a Captain, Too."

3: More seriously, a plea in the congressional record from 14 World War veterans of Johnstown, Pa. that committees of Senate and House investigate the award of captaincies to Elliott (in the specialists' reserve of the Air Corps) and to his older brother James (in the Marine Corps.)

The Johnstown veterans wrote:

"The undersigned ex-service men protest that the commissioning of the Roosevelt sons is unfair to the millions of American ex-soldiers who served in the country's armed forces in past wars, and to the young American manhood now awaiting the country's call to duty on Oct. 16, 1940."

RECALL WILLKIE

That is the day for registration of an estimated 11,000,000 men between 21 and 35 for training under the selective service law.

The Johnstown petitioners also said:

"Twenty-three years ago another young man had an opportunity to serve his country. On the day war was declared against Germany by the United States this young man and two brothers signed up for "the duration."

"This young man, Wendell Willkie, asked no favors—in fact he had no one to go to for political preferment to smooth his way in army service. He enlisted in the American way, served in a combat unit in the American way, and earned promotion in the American way—under fire."

LIVE WITH CONSCIENCE

In Fort Worth, Tex., Elliott Roosevelt said Saturday night he joined the Army because "I must live with my conscience."

"I recently decided one member of the Roosevelt family should show a concrete interest in the defense commission and I decided to join the Army," the President's second son said.

"I volunteered for any job and they commissioned me a captain in the air corps. Instead of doing something good as I thought I found I had committed a horrible political error.

"I had done one more thing to convince father that I always put my foot in my mouth. But I must live with my conscience."

Meanwhile, officers at Wright Field in Dayton said today that Captain Roosevelt would report Wednesday for active duty. Previously, he had been scheduled to report today.

When I was a boy I served a term
As account exec. of a big ad firm.
I didn't clean the windows nor sweep the floor
Nor polish up the handle of the big front door;
But I polished up my spurs so carefullee
That now I'm a Captain in the Air Armee!

In selling ads I made such a name
That Hearst's air editor I soon became;
The Texas air braced me to such a pink
That I stirred the ozone for Texas Network, Inc.
And what I learned about air so suited me
That now I'm a Captain in the Air Armee!

As account exec. I showed such bent
That they made me the new vice president.
Soon my voice sailed the ether, like pop's, so bland—
But I gave Brother Garner a great big hand.
Oh, I handed it to him so gallantlee
That now I'm a Captain in the Air Armee!

On atmospheric knowledge I acquired such a grip
That soon they awarded me a partnership.
This aerial experience in partnership, I ween,
Was about the only airship that I ever had seen
But that kind of ship so suited me
That now I'm the Captain of the Air Armee!

—With apologies to Gilbert and Sullivan

The next day, after the captain's arrival I escorted him to see Captain Gus Neece, our medical officer, for his physical examination. While that was going on I was attending to the care of Roosevelt's Texas hat and boots.

Two days later, Elliott's father, the president, visited Wright Field. Colonel York directed me to assemble all officers in front of the flag pole and get them in formation for a review by the president. I went to the gate at the entrance where I could witness the approach of the president and his retinue. As the group neared the entrance I rushed over to the area where the officers were gathering and, getting into the center of the group, directed them to align themselves on my position, to my right and left. Directly in front of me, about ten paces, was the Adjutant, Colonel John Y. York, Jr. [later major general].

We faced the flag pole and the automobile in which the president sat as he reviewed the officers and talked with those in his automobile.

They were Orville Wright, the airplane inventor, former Governor Cox of Ohio and Generals George Brett and Oliver Echols, our division commander.

After the party departed, I proceeded to the gate and was the first one to leave as the vehicles returned to the highway. See the following pictures. [Arrow on following photo identifies the author.]

Several days later, on the fourteenth, public and media furor over Elliott's appointment led the captain to submit his resignation to General Echols, our commanding general. The general refused it, stating that he needed his services.

The captain and I had periodic contacts while he was stationed at the field. I remember on January 18, 1941, he called me and wrote me concerning the case of a J. C. H. Stearns, an official of the Dow Chemical Company, who was about to be called to active duty as a reserve officer. The company wanted to get a deferment because he held a key position in coordinating all orders from the aircraft industry to his company and was trying to prevent possible delays in delivering aircraft orders for magnesium castings—magnesium being in very short supply. I carried the ball in getting this accomplished.

President Franklin D. Roosevelt, Wright Field, Ohio, 12 Oct. 1940.

Officers aligned on me, to my right and to my left since I was the assistant adjutant. The adjutant, Lieutenant Colonel John Y. York, is in front of the officers. I am behind him in the front row center. See black dot.

Courtesy WFPL

Salute to President Franklin D. Roosevelt, Wright Field, Ohio, 12 Oct. 1940. Officers aligned on me as I was the assistant adjutant, Wright Field, Ohio.

Courtesy WFPL

Back seat: President Roosevelt, Orville Wright, Former Governor Cox of Ohio, General Oliver Echols.
Front seat: General G. H. Brett, Wright Field, Ohio, 12 Oct. 1940.

Courtesy WFPL

A few months later Roosevelt had a desire to get out from behind an office desk and get into flying activities. He was able to get assigned to a reconnaissance aviation school for training. He progressed in this area of air intelligence, was promoted, and given command of a reconnaissance group and later a wing, achieving the rank of brigadier general. I recall one day he landed three of his aircraft at Patterson Field, which adjoins Wright Field. It was my duty to deliver to him some classified documents. I went over to the flight lines, delivered the documents and he showed me thru his plane. He called the three planes Jingle, Jangle, Jingle. I noticed with interest that he had three spurs, the kind that are attached to a horseman's boot heel, that were dangling down from the ceiling of the plane's cockpit above the pilot's head. [Symbolic, I presume, for urging the aircraft to speed into action.]

In August 1951, I was en route to California on my way overseas for duty in Alaska. I took the California Zephyr train out of Chicago. When the train stopped in Denver, into my Vista Dome car there came Elliott Roosevelt and his family, also en route to California. We had a nice chat and I took some pictures. Below is one of the family seated just in front of me in the car. Later I sent the pictures to their home in Hyde Park, NY.

Although Elliott served as an aide to his father during much of his service, he mollified to a great degree the criticism leveled at him earlier in the war. He flew eighty-nine missions, was twice wounded and was decorated for valor by four nations. The following Richmond Times Dispatch *article of October 28, 1990, provides a brief summary of his varied career.*

Elliott Roosevelt, author, dies at 80

SCOTTSDALE, Ariz. (AP) — Author Elliott Roosevelt, who served his father, President Franklin Roosevelt, during World War II and later wrote a best seller about it, died yesterday in Scottsdale.

He died of congestive heart failure at his home, said Patricia Roosevelt, his wife of 30 years.

Mr. Roosevelt, 80, was a World War II air force general as well as an author and lecturer. He was also a former mayor of Miami Beach, Fla., and a Democratic National Committeeman from that state.

His business career included ventures in advertising, radio station management and ranching.

Mr. Roosevelt was born Sept. 23, 1910, in New York. He attended Groton and Hun preparatory schools as well as Columbia University.

In World War II, Mr. Roosevelt commanded the multinational aerial reconnaissance wing that played a key role in the Allies' 1944 D-Day landings in Normandy, France, as well as the invasions of North Africa and Sicily.

He flew 89 missions, was wounded twice and was decorated for valor by the United States, France, Morocco and Britain.

Mr. Roosevelt launched his writing career in 1946 with the publication of the best-selling "As He Saw It," which detailed his experiences as aide to his father at five historic wartime summit conferences.

He later wrote a trilogy of books about his parents and in 1983 wrote "The Conservators," a statement of his philosophy about survival of the planet.

B. Major James H. Doolittle [later general]

AWARDED THE MEDAL OF HONOR AND THE MEDAL OF FREEDOM

During the early months of America's war effort, Major James Doolittle worked closely with the contract and production officials of our command in liaison with aircraft manufacturers of engines, equipment and parts to speed up the production of the weapons of war.

At many of his meetings at Wright Field with these officers he would come to see me about getting officers for duty at various aircraft facilities and elsewhere throughout the country. He always had a small black note book in his hand with names of officers or positions that he wanted to fill with men of special qualifications. I was glad to be able to furnish a number of good men to meet his needs. We in the adjutant's office issued all official orders, travel orders, etc. We were constantly issuing official travel orders for Doolittle who was flying to cities all over the country–hard to keep up with his movements.

The spectacular career of the Hero of the Tokyo Air Raid is provided in the following article that appeared in the Richmond Times Dispatch *in 1993:*

General James H. Doolittle

Hero of Tokyo raid Jimmy Doolittle dies

Inspirational World War II aviator was 96

THE ASSOCIATED PRESS

PEBBLE BEACH, Calif. — Retired Gen. James H. Doolittle, whose daring, daylight bombing raid on Japan during World War II stunned the Japanese and lifted American morale, has died at age 96.

Gen. Doolittle died Monday in the home of one of his sons. He had suffered a stroke earlier this month.

He set a string of aviation records in the 1920s and 1930s, as an Army pilot and then as an employee of Shell Oil Co.

But he was remembered above all for the first bombing raid of the war on Japan, on April 18, 1942.

Gen. Doolittle

The raid inflicted no major damage. A later Naval War College study could find no serious strategic reason for it.

But it stirred U.S. morale, just four months after Pearl Harbor, and put the Japanese on notice that their cities were in reach of U.S. air power. Spencer Tracy played Gen. Doolittle in the 1944 film "Thirty Seconds Over Tokyo."

'The master of the calculated risk'

When President Bush gave Gen. Doolittle the Presidential Medal of Freedom in 1989, he described him as "the master of the calculated risk." Gen. Doolittle also won the Medal of Honor.

Shortly after the war, he told a Senate committee: "You can't lose a war if you have command of the air, and you can't win a war if you haven't."

Gen. Doolittle was born in Alameda, Calif., and spent part of his early childhood in Alaska, where his father was a gold prospector. He attended Los Angeles Junior College and the University of California.

After the United States entered World War I in 1917, he enlisted in the Army. He earned his wings in 1918, but the war ended before he saw duty in France. He stayed on in the Army air service.

In 1922, he flew from Jacksonville, Fla., to Rockwell Field, near San Diego, in 22 hours and 30 minutes total elapsed time, stopping only briefly. It was the first coast-to-coast flight in less than 24 hours and earned him the Distinguished Flying Cross.

He set many flight records

In the Schneider Cup competition in 1925, he flew 232.573 mph, a record for a seaplane in a closed course. His "blind" instrument flight, in 1929, helped show the value of scientific vs. seat-of-the-pants aviation.

In 1930, he took a post at Shell's aviation fuel division. He continued competitive flying to help promote Shell and aviation in general. Later, he concentrated on improving the safety and reliability of aviation.

In 1931, he won the Bendix Trophy Race from Burbank to Cleveland, then continued on to the East Coast, setting another coast-to-coast record: 11 hours, 16 minutes, or almost half his record of a decade before.

While retaining his Army commission, he studied at Massachusetts Institute of Technology and earned a doctorate in aeronautical engineering in 1925.

After war broke out in Europe, Gen. Doolittle returned to active duty.

In 1942, he and fellow aviators were put aboard an aircraft carrier with 16 B-25 bombers for a special mission across the Pacific. He had made a special plea to be allowed to command the mission personally.

Squadron forced to take off early

The plan for the attack on Tokyo called for launching the planes just before dark, 500 miles from the Japanese coast. But while still 650 miles from the target, the Navy flotilla encountered Japanese patrol boats. Adm. William F. Halsey, fearing that surprise had been lost, ordered the B-25s to take off at once.

The bombers sought out military and industrial targets in Tokyo, in the naval ports of Yokohama and Yokosuka, and in three other cities in the Japanese heartland.

After the raid, the Doolittle raiders were to land at airfields in China. But the early takeoff, coupled with strong head winds, depleted their fuel, and almost all had to bail out.

Three men drowned or were killed when they parachuted. Eight landed in Japanese-held China and were imprisoned, three later to be executed and a fourth to die in prison.

But Gen. Doolittle and 68 others came down in free China or the Soviet Union and eventually made their way back to U.S. forces.

He went on to serve a variety of posts in the war, including commander of the Algeria-based 12th Air Force, and later the 8th Air Force, based in Britain, which blasted away Germany's air power. By the end of the war, he was the youngest lieutenant general in the Army.

President Reagan promoted him to four-star general in the Air Force Reserve in 1985.

After the war, Gen. Doolittle returned to Shell but remained active in speaking out about the military.

He quit flying in the late 1950s, saying, "I saw what happened to my friends who only half quit. They flew less and less and didn't stay proficient. Inevitably, they would be tempted to go into bad weather and they ended up dead."

He will be buried Friday beside his wife of 71 years, Josephine, at Arlington National Cemetery. She died in 1988.

They had two sons, James H. Jr. and John. Both became Air Force pilots.

C. James Stewart [later brigadier general]

Our Command Motion Picture Unit which was responsible for making motion pictures for the Air Corps was making an effort to get Jimmy Stewart, the movie actor, assigned to the Air Corps.

In order to do so we had to provide Headquarters, Army Air Corps, Washington, D.C., with justification and a proposed duty assignment.

Below is a self-explanatory teletype message from Air Corps Headquarters and my teletype message in reply.

```
                        C O P Y

                                Received   March 19, 1941.

E-181    3-19-41

ADMINISTRATIVE EXECUTIVE

ATTENTION:  CAPTAIN JOHN H. FITE

RETELETYPE DHQ-T-334, DATED 3-18-41, REFERENCE CASE OF JAMES STEWART,

REQUEST ADDITIONAL INFORMATION BE FURNISHED IN ORDER THAT A GOOD CASE

CAN BE BUILT UP IN FAVOR OF HAVING JAMES STEWART ASSIGNED TO THE AIR

CORPS.  TO WHAT ORGANIZATION SHOULD HE BE ASSIGNED?  STATE NAMES OF SOME

OF THE PICUTRES IN WHICH HE HAS PLAYED IN CCOPERATION WITH THE AIR CORPS.

EXECUTIVE

HP

10:45 AM
```

```
MDAC-5-WF-9-12-40-75M                              WDS:BM

                TELETYPE  MESSAGE

PRIORITY                                DATE:  MARCH 19, 1941
                    3:00 P.M.
                                        FROM   ADJUTANTS OFFICE


ATTENTION:      EXECUTIVE


PHQ-T-357          RETEL E 181 DATED MARCH 19, 1941 REFERENCE CASE OF JAMES

STEWART RECOMMEND THAT HE BE ENLISTED IN HEADQUARTERS SQUADRON 50TH TRANSPORT

WING WRIGHT FIELD DAYTON, OHIO.  HE CAN BE USED IN THE FORTHCOMING SCHOOL OF

AVIATION MEDICINE PICTURE, AND WILL BE USED IN SUBJECTS IN OTHER PICTURES ON

FIGHTERS, LIGHT AND HEAVY BOMBERS AS WELL AS ASSISTING IN DIRECTING THESE PICTURES

AND AS COMMENTATOR FOR SAME.  IT IS XXXX BELIEVED THAT HIS SERVICES IN THIS

CAPACITY, IN VIEW OF HIS BACKGROUND AND EXPERIENCE, IN THE MOTION PICTURE INDUSTRY

WOULD STIMULATE INTEREST IN THE PROPOSED MOTION PICTURE PROGRAM.


                            ADMINISTRATIVE EXECUTIVE
```

In August 1994 I sent copies of these messages to Jimmy Stewart along with a letter. A copy of his reply is shown below.

JAMES STEWART

August 16, 1994

Walbrook D. Swank
RR2 Box 433
Col, USAF (Ret)
Mineral, VA 23117

Dear Colonel Swank:

Regretfully, Mr. Stewart is not in good health and is unable to personally respond to your letter.

Mr. Stewart asked me to write to you and thank you for sending the copies of the teletype messages and for the lovely letter you wrote to him.

Mr. Stewart wanted you to know that he is grateful to you for thinking of him and he sends you his best wishes.

Sincerely,

Sharon Margulies
Secretary to James Stewart

SM/ms

D. Lieutenant General William Knudsen

Head of Production, US Army [formerly chairman, War Production Board].

On March 9, 1942, General Knudsen met with Gen. Arthur Vanaman, our commanding general, and from five to six in the evening I participated in the discussions. My input related to manpower, deferment and staffing problems. The general toured the installation and reviewed the various engineering, research, development and production activities. See newspaper article below:

GEN. KNUDSEN, ON TOUR HERE, SATISFIED WITH PRODUCTION

Left to right: Lt. Col. Walter G. Bain, Wright Field; Maj. William Collins, executive officer for Lt. Gen. William Knudsen; Gen. Knudsen, head of production, United States army; Col. Fred McMahon, Cincinnati district army ordnance chief.

E. Charles A. Lindbergh [later brigadier general]

On 28 May 1943 Charles Lindbergh met with Brig. Gen. Charles E. Branshaw [later major general]. Our commanding general and I took part in the discussions concerning manpower, staffing deferment and personnel management problems within the command. While at the base Lindbergh reviewed the activities in the research, engineering and production units. In 1941 he testified before Congress against the Land-Lease Act and believed in neutrality in the war. He resigned his commission in the US Army Reserve Corps after President Roosevelt criticized him for his anti-war attitudes. Following the United States' entry into the war he worked as a technical advisor to military aircraft manufacturers. In 1944 the War Department sent him to combat commands in the Pacific to study the performance of P-38 twin-engine fighter planes. He participated in about fifty missions in action against the Japanese.

Following the war Lindbergh served as a consultant to the chief of staff, US Air Force and was commissioned a brigadier general in the Air Force Reserve in 1954.

F. Captain Russell Montgomery

A depressing assignment was given to me on 24 February 1941 when my boss, Colonel John Y. York, detailed me to escort the remains of Captain Russell Montgomery, an aeronautical engineer, to his home in Scotsburg, Indiana. He and another Air Force officer were badly burned and killed when their airplane crashed and exploded on a ridge near Athens, Ohio, en route to Wright Field.

The captain's parents, John and Carrie Montgomery, invited me to stay in their son's room in their home and asked me to read the obituary at the services held at the Stewart Memorial Funeral Home. Russell had two brothers. One, Willard, was a first lieutenant in the Army Medical Corps and stationed in Texas. He could not arrive in time for the funeral because his plane was delayed by bad weather. The Montgomerys were a prominent family in the town, and the funeral home was filled to capacity.

At the brief services at the cemetery I presented the American flag that covered the casket to Mrs. Montgomery. She treated me like a son and gave me a pair of her son's cuff links and some weeks later sent me a beautiful afghan she had made. [See the following picture.] Willard arrived in time for the graveside service. In private practice before the war he was a technical consultant to the director of the TV program "Dr. Kildare."

We kept in touch with the Montgomerys for many years.

The author beside the casket.
Captain Montgomery's picture is to the right.

Afghan given by Mrs. Montgomery to the author.

PART 2

HQ, AAF Midcentral Procurement District, Chicago, Illinois

The exemplary manner in which this command contributed to the war effort and striking power of the American Air Force is well expressed in the following letter from General H. H. Arnold, commanding general, Army Air Forces.

A. Letter from Commanding General, Army Air Forces.

ARMY AIR FORCES
HEADQUARTERS OF THE MATERIEL COMMAND

WRIGHT FIELD, DAYTON, OHIO
15 October 1943

Subject: Congratulations.

To: Midcentral Procurement District Supervisor
111 W. Jackson Blvd.
Chicago 4, Illinois

     1. There is quoted below for your information and such dissemination as you desire, a letter dated 15 October 1943 from the Commanding General, Army Air Forces:

"Major General Charles E. Branshaw
Commanding General
Army Air Forces Materiel Command

My dear General Branshaw:

     On October 15, 1926, the Materiel Division, Air Corps, was activated at Dayton, Ohio. Today, I send you and all personnel of the Materiel Command heartiest congratulations from the rest of the Army Air Forces.

     The important part played by this organization during the past seventeen years, and particularly during our great expansion program, is fully realized and has definitely contributed to the successes we are now enjoying. The work you are doing to supply our Air Forces with the very best equipment available is most vital to the war effort of this country. It is only by diligence and conscientious effort on the part of every single officer, enlisted man and civilian employee that we can be assured of ultimate victory which will hasten the day when those we love will be returned to their homes.

     Keep up the good work and the very best of luck to all of you in the days to come.

                    Very sincerely,

                    /s/ H. H. ARNOLD
                    General, U. S. Army
              Commanding General, Army Air Forces."

2. Such success as the Materiel Command has had in performing its functions is due in great measure to the general excellence of the work being performed for these headquarters by the Procurement Districts. I therefore take this means of commending all your personnel, both military and civilian, who have contributed in any measure to the success of our Command.

CHAS. E. BRANSHAW
Major General, U.S.A.
Commanding

Subj: Congratulations

1st Ind.

AMD:rr

War Dept., Army Air Forces, Materiel Command, Office of the District Supervisor, Midcentral Procurement District, 111 W. Jackson Blvd., Chicago 4, Illinois, 19 October 1943.

TO: All military and civilian personnel of the Midcentral Procurement District.

1. It is a source of great satisfaction to add my congratulations to those of General Arnold and General Branshaw to all military and civilian personnel of the Midcentral Procurement District for their individual efforts in accomplishing an outstanding job.

2. Keep it up!

Alonzo M. Drake
Colonel, Air Corps
District Supervisor

B. Presentation of Awards

I was appointed to present awards to the next of kin of Air Force members who had been killed, were missing in action or taken prisoner, and had been awarded a decoration which they were unable to accept.

On June 21, 1944, I presented three medals to parents of a Swedish captain and Jewish lieutenant who were killed in action.

Articles about these two presentations appeared in the Chicago Heights *newspaper and are shown below.*

WIFE IS PRESENTED HERO'S AIR MEDAL

The wife and four-month-old son (Michael Allan) of Lieutenant Roy P. Stealey were the center of attention at the Chicago Heights Rotary club's meeting when army officers presented the Air Medal won by Lieut. Stealey, now a prisoner of war in Germany. The wife is the former Virginia Lee Hansen, 33 East Twenty-fourth street. Others in the picture are Major W. D. Swank of the Army Air Forces, who made the presentation and Captain F. J. Leahy and Sergeant W. T. Hurley, both of District 3, Sixth Service Command. The ceremony was the first public event of its kind here during the current war.

HEROISM EARNS AWARD

HEROISM IN AIR COMBAT was recognized in a ceremony this week in Chicago Heights. Top photo, Major W. D. Swank of the Army Air Forces presents to Mrs. Josephine Rauba, 1620 Portland avenue, the Distinguished Flying Cross earned by her son, Staff Sergeant Anthony J. Rauba, in the raid August 1 on the Ploesti oil refineries of Rumania. Sergeant Rauba is now a prisoner of war in Rumania. Others in the picture are (left to right) Sergeant W. T. Hurley, Mrs. Aldo Paci (sister of Sergeant Rauba) and Captain F. W. Leahy. The presentation was made on Tuesday at the Rauba home through arrangements made by headquarters of District 3, Sixth Service Command.

Dec. 21, 1943

C. War Bond Drives

AAF Midcentral Procurement District

    As an additional duty I was District War Bond Officer and developed a promotion program throughout our five state region to attain full participation in the bond drives by all of our personnel.

    The items below reflect the extent of participation in the Fourth War Bond Drive by MCPD personnel.

Major W. D. Swank discusses 4th War Loan Drive with Jack Kindall, President, MCPD Welfare Association, Feb. 9, 1944.

4TH WAR BOND DRIVE EXTENDED TO FEB. 29 FOR WAR DEPT. EMPLOYEES

WAR LOAN DRIVE EXTENDED...MCPD REACHING GOAL

The Fourth War Loan Drive which ended national-
ly today has been extended in the War Department
until February 29. Major W. D. Swank, District
War Bond Officer, released the figures for the

Organization	Civilian Participation	Civilian Payroll	Civ. and Mil. Cash Sales
MCPD Headquarters	74. %	5.8%	$31,812.00
Chicago Area	61. %	5.1%	$ 9,918.00
Indianapolis Area	79.1%	7.9%	$ 5,005.00
South Bend Area	67.5%	5.2%	$ 9,222.00
Milwaukee Area	85. %	7.2%	$ 1,562.00
Minneapolis Area	88. %	7.7%	$ 9,230.00
GFE Depot	74. %	5.0%	$12,075.00
Average	72.5%	6.2%	
		Total	$78,824.00

month of January of the progress of the MCPD War
Loan Drive and expressed confidence that the MCPD
goal of 90 per cent participation in the Payroll
Reservation Plan and 10 per cent deductions of
gross pay would be achieved by the conclusion of
the drive.

UNITED STATES TREASURY DEPARTMENT

For distinguished services rendered in behalf of the
War Bond Program, this citation is awarded to

Major W. D. Swank

Given under my hand and seal on March 21, 1946.

Fred M. Vinson

Secretary of the Treasury

D. Wartime Labor Shortages

Labor shortages in the five states comprising our procurement district were so acute that the War Manpower Commission took steps to ration available manpower, or adjust or withdraw war contracts in Illinois, Wisconsin and Indiana. Of the 72 Group I areas of critical labor shortages throughout the United States in March 1944, 18 or 25 percent of the total were in the three-state region.

An extreme example of the impact of this manpower problem is vividly portrayed in the newspaper article on the right.

This event took place across the street from my office!

Chicago Herald-American
★★★★ Mon., Apr. 17, 1944—3

Can't Hire Help, Dies in Leap

A La Salle st. insurance executive, brooding over the manpower shortage that had depleted his staff, ended his life today by leaping from a window of his 18th floor suite in the Board of Trade Building, 316 S. La Salle st.

He was Grover H. Garretson, 55, of 9043 S. Laflin st., district manager for the General Accident, Fire & Life Assurance Company. His body narrowly missed several pedestrians as it hurtled to the La Salle st. sidewalk.

Sgt. John Steiner of central police found $220 in Garretson's wallet along with a note, apparently addressed to his main office, which read:

"Please arrange to take over my agency at once. Cannot get help to handle business. Resigning, will protect business until your representative arrives and make a full accounting of all collections. Urgent."

Miss Annette Green, 5132 S. Western av., Garretson's secretary, entered the office at 8 a. m. She noticed the opened window, and at this point a mailman entered and told of seeing a man's broken body on the walk below.

The secretary and Mrs. Florence Garretson, the widow, gave police similar reports of the insurance executive's extreme worry over business cares, particularly his failure to find replacements for workers called to war.

Also surviving are two daughters, Mrs. Muriel Stallard and Mrs. Edna Koenig.

One of the major problems in our command was the recruitment and manning of aircraft inspector, technical and clerical positions in the many aircraft and equipment manufacturing facilities in our district.

Apropos to this problem I sent the following cartoon to many of our operating officials!

NUTS AND JOLTS   By Bill Holman

The employment agency sent him over last week. That's all they had.

YOURS FOR BETTER EMPLOYEE UTILIZATION IN 1944

W. T. SWANK
Major, A.C.
Civilian Personnel Officer

Part 3

HQ, Pacific Overseas Air Technical Service Command, Oakland/Alameda, California

Headquarters Building, Alameda, Calif., Pacific Overseas Air Technical Service Command. *Courtesy POATSCPL*

Courtesy POATSCPL

Brigadier General William E. Farthing
Based on Brigadier General Farthing's recommendation I received the Army Commendation Medal for Outstanding Performance of Duty as Chief, Personnel and Training Division, HQ, Pacific Overseas Air Technical Command on 4 February 1940.

Return of war-damaged aircraft for reconditioning from Pacific overseas area. Shipside at Alameda.
Courtesy POATSCPL

Shipment of equipment and supplies to Pacific overseas areas. Wharf at Alameda.
Courtesy POATSCPL

Pfc. Robert Winslow showing Miss Lola See holes in a captured Japanese airplane at Oakland Municipal Airport.

Courtesy POATSCPL

My wife, Janie, and I at "Lookout Point," San Francisco, Calif., 1946.

A. Alcatraz Island, Federal Prison

Captain Edward J. Bennett, one of my assistants, asked me if I would like to tour Alcatraz Federal Prison on Alcatraz Island in San Francisco Bay. His father was the director of all US Federal prisons. We both thought it was a good idea, so he made arrangements for the trip. On the 24th of May 1945 we took a motor launch at the wharf at San Francisco for Alcatraz Island which is a twelve-acre rock rising above the water in the bay.

The prison housed about two hundred and fifty of the most hardened criminals in the nation. The average sentence was thirty-two years. We saw Robert Stroud, the famous "Bird Man of Alcatraz," who became a leading expert on bird diseases; the notorious "Machine Gun" Kelly; Al Karpis; and a German saboteur.

We were told that the prisoners had to line up and take a shower twice a week, whether they liked it or not, and if they caused no trouble they could visit the library. Travel magazines and books were read the most. The warden said they were all "dog eared."

Following the tour the warden invited us to lunch in his lovely dining room with a beautiful view of the San Francisco Bay area, bridges and mountains. The waiter was a prisoner with a life sentence.

A few months later in 1946, there was a bloody riot and an escape attempt by the inmates. See the following newspaper account of the plot and the death of the last convict survivor of the revolt [Richmond News Leader, October 5, 1988].

Survivor of Alcatraz plot dies

By The Associated Press

SPRINGFIELD, Mo. — Clarence Carnes, the only inmate survivor of a 1946 escape attempt from Alcatraz that left seven dead, has died in prison, a month before he was to be released.

Carnes died Monday at the Medical Center for Federal Prisoners. He was 61 and had spent most of his life behind bars.

On July 6, 1945, Carnes was sent to Alcatraz, the federal prison island in San Francisco Bay. He was 18, the youngest inmate to be incarcerated there.

Early the next year, Carnes was drawn into a daring escape plot that quickly went awry. Two guards were killed and several wounded. The six inmates who participated got control of little more than one cell house.

Marines on their way home from Okinawa helped prison guards called from as far away as Leavenworth, Kan., retake the prison.

When it was over, three inmates were dead. Two others, Miran Edgar Thompson and Sam Shockley, were later executed. Carnes was spared the death penalty because he had refused when assigned to kill several guards.

For six years Carnes was confined to a cell next to one occupied by Robert Stroud, the Birdman of Alcatraz. Stroud had donated $200 to the defense fund for Carnes, Shockley and Thompson from royalties from his book, "Digest of Bird Diseases."

Carnes, born to impoverished Indian parents in eastern Oklahoma, committed his first crime at age 8 by stealing candy bars at school.

In 1943 he was sentenced to life in prison after he pleaded guilty to murdering an Oklahoma service station attendant during a holdup.

In 1963, four months before Alcatraz was closed as a prison, Carnes was transferred to Springfield and then to Leavenworth in January 1963.

In October 1970 he was paroled to Oklahoma, where he still had time to serve on the murder sentence.

Carnes was released to federal parole on Dec. 21, 1973. He lived in the Kansas City area after that, but his parole was revoked twice for minor infractions, mostly because of a drinking problem. He was to be released from prison again next month.

B. Return of Admiral William F. "Bull" Halsey's Third Fleet.

The 26th of October 1945 was celebrated as "Navy Day" in the San Francisco Bay area as Admiral William F. "Bull" Halsey's Third Fleet, returning from the war in the Pacific, sailed into the bay. Japanese officials signed the surrender terms on Halsey's flagship, the Missouri.

Following the Japanese cease-fire on 15 August 1945, he is said to have ordered all Japanese snooper planes to be shot down, "not in a spirit of vengeance, but in a friendly fashion."

I, along with several other officers, sailed around the bay viewing the ceremonies and various ships from the motor launch pictured below.

Also shown are pictures of the battleships Wisconsin *and* South Dakota *and the light cruiser* Oakland.

South Dakota

Wisconsin

Oakland

C. Announcement of the Death of President Roosevelt.

FROM SHEDD CG NSC FORT DOUGLAS UTAH 132204Z

TO CG PAC OVERSEAS ATSC OAKLAND CALIF

    GRNC

The following War Department radio is repeated for information "GO 29 War Department, Washington DC 13 April 1945.   1. The following order of the
honorable Henry L. Stimson, Secretary of War, announces to the Army the death
of Franklin Delano Roosevelt, President of the United States: "It is my duty
as Secretary of War to announce to the Army the death of Franklin Delano
Roosevelt, President of the United States, which occurred at Warm Springs,
Georgia at 1635 hours 12 April 1945. The Army is deeply grieved at the
untimely death of our Commander in Chief. He prepared us to meet the savage
onslaught of our enemies and he led us through the bitterness of our early
reversals. His unwavering courage in the face of overwhelming odds, his
abiding faith in the final triumph of Democratic ideals and his clear vision
of the paths to be followed were a source of constant inspiration. He gave
the Army unstintedly of his strength and wisdom, and his unremitting labors
hastened his death. Although he leaves us while there is still much hard
fighting ahead the ultimate victory has been fashioned of his heart and spirit.
Memorial services shall be held on the day of the funeral, 15 April, at all
posts, camps and stations, war operations permitting, at which time this order
will be read. The former Vice President of the United States, Harry S. Truman,
has taken the Oath of Office and assumed the duty of President in accordance
with the provisions of the Constitution." 2. The National flag will be dis-
played at half staff at the Headquarters of all military commands and vessels
under the control of the War Department from 0800 hours local time, 13 April
1945 until sunset 12 May 1945 west longitude dates operations permitting. The
wearing of mourning bands, the draping of colors and standards and the firing of
salutes will be dispensed with because of war conditions. 3. The body of the
late commander in chief will be interred at Hyde Park, N.Y. on 15 April 1945.
By order of the Secretary of War: G.C. Marshall, Chief of Staff.

PART 4

SUNDRIES

(1) A News Release from England

The following is an astonishing news story released in England about safeguarding military information:

SAFEGUARDING MILITARY INFORMATION

A news story released from England relates the following:

A 19 year old inmate of a youth correction institution escaped wearing shorts and a singlet. After talking to a sympathetic sailor he obtained a suit of green fatigues and drove away in a stolen Naval vehicle.

Later in London he exchanged the Naval vehicle for a jeep and entered a military area by means of a trip ticket left in the jeep. An unattended room provided access to more military clothing in which he dressed and later borrowed money from one of the personnel at the establishment.

He returned to London, struck up an acquaintance with an American officer who offered to share his lodging with him. The officer awoke the next morning to find a uniform missing.

Arriving at an airport this youth represented himself as a Rail Transportation officer and got a ride aboard a military plane without being asked for identification. In Edinburgh he visited the Red Cross and stole a wallet containing money and identity papers of an American Army officer. At a Royal Air Force airport he had his picture taken by an official photographer and attached this to the stolen AGO card. Travelling to the nearest Finance Office he presented the stolen pay card plus a chit which he had typed and received a pay advance. Calling "Operations" he was accepted as co-pilot on a plane returning to London.

Enroute to London the Officer of the Day at an intermediate field requested him to deliver an official mail pouch which he carried to Headquarters in London.

Attaching himself to a party of high ranking officers and representing himself as the Public Relations Officer, he accompanied the official party to France and returned by the same plane.

Calling at the RTO's office at a London Railway station he was permitted to enter and taking advantage of the situation he made out several free travel warrants, one of which he used to go to Northingham.

Next morning he was flown to Hendon after showing the stolen AGO card. At Mail Distribution he declared himself an Officer Courier and asked for a jeep. He was referred to SHAEF and was successful in obtaining transportation. While waiting for the jeep, he typed a permit for himself as an officer on confidential duty and forged the name of the Commanding General of the Allied Forces.

After reaching London he called the New Scotland Yard and inquired into the record of his real self. No information was given over the phone but a personal interview was arranged for the following day.

When he went to Mail Distribution the next morning he was apprehended. His career as an Army man, assumed 22 June 1944, ended 25 July.

This true story was carried in American papers six months ago. Laughable and amusing as it is, before you take a superior attitude, ask yourself --

How many times have I accepted a person arriving at this Headquarters merely on their statement?

How many times have I shown confidential material to someone in uniform because they asked to see it without ascertaining whether or not it was in accordance with paragraph 11, AR 380-5?

How often have I left papers around that could be taken and forged?

Am I over-trustful and not suspicious enough?

THIS CAN HAPPEN IN THIS COMMAND!

SAFEGUARD MILITARY INFORMATION!

(2) A General is Disciplined.

The following is an unusual incident in which the Commanding General of the Army Air Forces disciplines a general officer for a deviation in military courtesy:

                                                           April 27, 1942

SUBJECT: Irregularity in Military Courtesy.

TO: Brigadier General K   B. W
            Through: Brigadier General Arthur Vanaman

      There is attached hereto a photograph allegedly taken in the vicinity of
Portland, Oregon, which, to all intents and purposes, shows that we have a
Brigadier General of the Air Corps who is not familiar with the basic knowledge of
a soldier. It is desired that this evidence be shown to General W   and that he
be directed to reply by indorsement hereon as to what action by the Commanding
General he believes is necessary to prevent a recurrence of this alleged irregularity
Authority for this posture cannot be located in the current series of Army Regulation

                                          H. H. ARNOLD
                                          Lieutenant General, U.S.A.
                                          Commanding General, Army Air Forces

1 Incl:
   Photograph.

                              1st Ind.

War Department, Army Air Forces, Materiel Center, Office of Commanding General,
Wright Field, Ohio, May 1, 1942 - To: Brigadier General K   B. W   U.S.A.

   1.   For necessary action.

                                          A. W. VANAMAN,
                                          Brigadier General, U.S.A.,
                                          Commanding General,
                                          AAF Materiel Center.

                              2nd Ind.

Brigadier General K   B. W   , U.S.A., Wright Field, Dayton, Ohio. May 1, 1942
To: Commanding General, Army Air Forces, Materiel Center.

   1.   The action taken by the Commanding General, Army Air Forces, in bringing to
the attention of the undersigned, this irregularity in military courtesy is sufficien
in itself to prevent any recurrence.

                                          K. B. W
                                          Brigadier General, U.S.A..

Enc- n/c

                              3rd Ind.

War Department, Army Air Forces, Materiel Center, Office of Commanding General, Wright
Field, Ohio, May 2, 1942 - To: Commanding General, Army Air Forces, Washington, D.C.

   1.   Forwarded.

                                          A. W. VANAMAN,
                                          Brigadier General, U.S.A.,
                                          Commanding General,
                                          AAF MATERIEL CENTER.

enc -n/c

(3) Marital Stress

Below is a copy of a letter to the Chief of the Air Force from a soldier's distraught wife regarding her marital relations.

Chief of the Air Force:-

Dear Sir:-

I know the way things are at present you may not want to be bothered reading anything that does not pertain to business but please take time before destroying this letter as we feel it very important to us at least.

We wives are trying awfully hard to take this war calmly and doing Red Cross work to take up some of our time when not busy with our families so that it's pretty hard to take when we know our husbands aren't on the up and up. We know for a fact that there are girls at the Field that are going with married men after working hours and the men use the excuse that they have to work over-time. We are willing and more than glad to have them work over-time in order to shorten this war but to have to share them with another woman is pretty hard to take.

We don't know if there is anything you can do about but we feel that if you would put a bulletin out to the effect that it is known that there are things going on out there that the guilty parties will at least get a scare and maybe stop this running around. We are sure that if any thing happened and the men would be needed at their desks sometime after leaving the Field that they would not be at home and if located would be in no condition to come to work. We can't help it anymore than our husbands that this war started but we are willing to stay at home with our children and give up all social functions and if we have to surely the other girls that are not married can leave hands off of our husbands. We had no trouble holding our husbands before but now they seem to think they have to stay out because they have to work so hard, well it's no fun at home either but we can take it.

Please destroy this letter immediately after you read it and please try to do something about it in order that we can be happy again.

                                   Thank you very much

(4) Marry Not an Engineer.

The lament of an engineer's sweetheart is well expressed in the words that follow:

THE TWENTY-THIRD PSALM OF AN ENGINEER'S SWEETHEART

Verily, I say unto you, marry not an engineer, for an engineer is a strange being and is possessed of many evils. Yes, he speaketh eternally in parables which he calleth formulas . . . he showeth always a serious aspect and seemeth not to know how to smile, and he picketh a seat in the car by the springs therein and not by the damsels. Verily though his damsel expecteth chocolates when he calleth, she opens the package to disclose samples of iron ore. Yes, he holdeth her hand to measure the friction therein, and he kisseth her only to test the viscosity of her lips. For in his eyes there shineth a faraway look that is neither love nor longing . . . rather a vain attempt to recall a formula. Even as a boy he pulleth a girl's hair but to test its elasticity. But as a man he discovereth different devices, for he counteth the vibrations of her heartstrings . . . his marriage will be simultaneous equation in two unknown yielding diverse results.

Sequel to the Wolf

If she throws her little "Quiver"
In the front seat of your fliver,
and says 'it's pleasant on the river'
Brother . . . she's a wolf.

If the get-up that she's wearing
Turns your head & keeps you staring
Cause the length's a little daring
Brother . . . she's a wolf.

If she is careless as can be
Sure enough she'll show her knee

You know there's a plenty else to see
Brother . . . she's a wolf.

If she really is bewitching
If she kisses with a twitching
As if her rosy lips were itching
Brother . . . she's a wolf.

If she really lets you pet her
Let's you snuggle in her sweater
And you really think you better
Brother . . . she's a wolf.

(5) Comments of Lovers?

Are the comments of lovers those painted in the lines that follow?

A soldier returning to camp after a two-week leave received this letter from his girl. She had written this little song for him.

M is for the many times you made me
O is for the other times you tried
T is for the tourist cabin weekends
H is for the Hell that is in your eyes.
E is for the everlasting love light
R is for the wreck you made of me
Put them all together they spell MOTHER, and brother, that's what I'm going to be.

The next day the soldier answered her letter and returned the compliment by dedicating this song to her.

F is for the funny little letter
A is for the answer to your note
T is for your tearful accusation
H is for the hope that I'm the goat
E is for the ease with which I made you
R is for Rube you thought I'd be
Put them all together they spell FATHER, but you're crazy if you think it's me.

(6) Does Destiny Dictate?

	<u>MUSSOLINI</u>	<u>STALIN</u>	<u>HITLER</u>	<u>ROOSEVELT</u>
Born	1883	1879	1889	1882
Came into power	1922	1924	1933	1933
Years in power	18	16	7	7
Age	57	61	51	58
Divided by 2:	3880	3880	3880	3880
Equals	1940	1940	1940	1940

<u>DON'T SELL YOUR BIRTHRIGHT FOR A MESS OF DICTATORS!</u>

Citizens Committee of One Thousand for WILLKIE
112 Park Avenue, Murray Hill Hotel
Lexington 2-2300, New York, New York

<u>VOTE FOR WILLKIE</u>

(7) Statistics

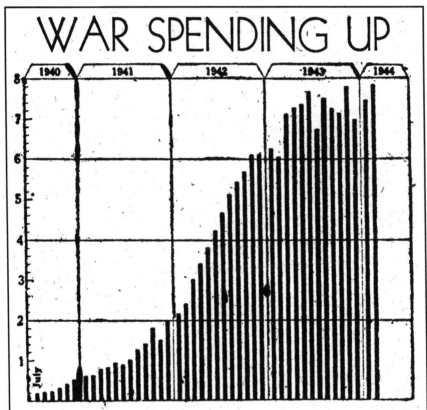

WAR SPENDING UP

War expenditures last month reached a new high of $7,800,000,-000, an increase of almost $400,-000,000 over January, according to the War Production Board. The previous high was $7,700,000,-000 in November of last year. The daily average of war spending in February rose to $312,000,000 from $285,000,000 in January. The above chart prepared by Dow-Jones traces the monthly fluctuations in war spending since July, 1940. The scale used represents billions of dollars.

* * * * * * *

ENEMY LOSES 29,316 PLANES IN THREE YEARS

In the three years since Pearl Harbor, the United States Army Air Forces dispatched 1,566,329 planes which dropped 1,202,139 tons of bombs on enemy targets, the War Department announced recently. During this period, a total of 29,316 enemy planes were destroyed.

Reflecting numerical and qualitative superiority over the enemy in all theaters, comparative AAF losses totaled 13,491 planes.

The Air Forces at the end of the war had lost about 22,900 planes, about 11,500 of them on combat missions. More than 40,000 enemy aircraft were destroyed.

At the peak of its manpower strength the United States Army Air Force was comprised of about 2,400,000 military personnel.

CASUALTIES IN WORLD WAR II

Country	Men in War	Battle Deaths	Wounded
Australia	1,000,000	26,976	180,864
Austria	800,000	280,000	350,117
Belgium	625,000	8,460	55,513
Bulgaria	340,000	6,700	21,900
Canada	1,040,000	32,400	53,145
China	17,250,000	1,324,500	1,762,000
Denmark	—	4,339	—
Finland	500,000	79,047	50,000
France	—	201,500	400,000
Germany	20,000,000	3,250,000	7,250,000
Greece	—	17,024	47,290
Hungary	—	147,435	89,313
India	2,400,000	32,000	64,350
Italy	3,100,000	149,500	66,716
Japan	9,700,000	1,270,000	140,000
Netherlands	280,000	6,500	2,860
New Zealand	194,000	11,625	17,000
Norway	75,000	2,000	—
Poland	—	664,000	530,000
Romania	650,000	350,000	—
South Africa, Union of	410,000	2,473	—
U.S.S.R.	—	6,115,000	14,012,000
United Kingdom	5,896,000	357,116	369,267
Yugoslavia	3,741,000	305,000	425,000
United States	16,112,566	291,557	670,846

(8) A GI Sign in the Pacific War Zone.

KILL THE BASTARDS! Down this road marched one of the regiments of the Unites States Army KNIGHTS SERVING THE QUEEN OF BATTLES. Twenty of their wounded in litters were bayoneted, shot and clubbed by the yellow bellies. KILL THE BASTARDS!

(9) "High Flight"

He Wrote War Masterpiece Before He Met His God

DESTINED TO BE ACCEPTED as one of the poetic masterpieces of the war is "High Flight."

It was written by an American flier serving with the Canadian Air Forces overseas—John G. Magee Jr.

Magee mailed the poem to his mother in Washington, D. C., but before it reached her she had the news of his death in an air fight.

Overnight "High Flight" became known. Air force men love it for its feeling of flying which they knew but could not describe. It runs:

HIGH FLIGHT

"Oh I have slipped the surly bonds of earth,
And danced the skies on laughter-silvereed wings;
Sunward, I've climbed and joined the tumbling mirth
Of sun-split clouds—and done a hundred things
You have not dreamed of—wheeled and snared and swung
High in the sunlit silence. Hov'ring there,
I've chased the shouting wind along and flung
My eager craft through footless halls of air.
Up, up the long delirious, burning blue
I've topped the wind-swept heights with easy grace.
Where never lark, or even eagle flew;
And while with silent, lifting mind I've trod
The high untrespassed sanctity of space,
Put out my hand, and touched the face of God."

HOTEL WINTHROP

TACOMA, WASHINGTON

(10) A Peril in the Night

Above is the letterhead of the stationery of the hotel I was in while on a staff visit to our Tacoma, Washington, Intransit Depot.

At 4:15 A.M. on October 5, 1945, a fire broke out on the fourth floor. The smoke came from the window of the room directly below my room. I was awakened by the sirens of the fire trucks and police cars on the street below my room. The firemen placed a round jump net below for people in the building to leap into from the upper floors. From the fifth floor it looked the size of a dime! A frightening experience. Smoke filled the hall outside the door to my room. Choosing not to take a chance and jump, I soon heard firemen in the hallway wielding their axes and trying to clear the smoke. In a short time we had access to the hall and the fire below had been contained.

It was reported that a returning Navy veteran in the room below apparently went to sleep with a lighted cigarette which caused the fire. He was seriously burned and taken to the hospital. The damage was estimated at $10,000,00.

(11) A Page from a War Ration Book.

578|444 BH

4

UNITED STATES OF AMERICA
OFFICE OF PRICE ADMINISTRATION

OFFICE OF PRICE
ADMINISTRATION

WAR RATION BOOK FOUR

Issued to *Walbrook W. Swank*
(Print first, middle, and last names)

Complete address *6966 N. Sheridan Ave*

Chicago - Ill

READ BEFORE SIGNING

In accepting this book, I recognize that it remains the property of the United States Government. I will use it only in the manner and for the purposes authorized by the Office of Price Administration.

Void if Altered   *Walbrook D. Swank*
(Signature)

It is a criminal offense to violate rationing regulations.

OPA Form R-145   16—35570-1

(12) Commission Seeker

As asst. administrative executive to the commanding general, AAF Materiel Center/Command, it was part of my officer's function to receive, evaluate and forward to appropriate operating officials the applications of people seeking a military commission and assignment to our command.

If the applicant possessed legal, executive, engineering or scientific experience the operating official needed, he would recommend the person's appointment and our office would process and forward a recommendation to HQ AAF for his appointment in the Specialist Reserve at an appropriate grade.

Below is a copy of an ambitious applicant's letter which is unique and of unusual interest. Note copy of my reply.

C O P Y

FAMOUS-BARR CO.   Saint Louis, Mo.

First in St. Louis.....Fifth in America

May 22, 1942.

Commanding Officer,
Personnel Procurement,
Army Air Corps,
Wright Field,
Dayton, Ohio.

Dear Sir:

I want the privilege of wearing this:

(2nd Lt. Bar - returned)

I don't want to be a General...or a Colonel...or a Major...or a Captain... or a First Lieutenant (now). All I'm asking is a Second Lieutenancy and I know I can make the grade. For eight long years I've had my nose to the grindstone in the Fifth Largest Retail Store in America. Because I'm a hard worker...I've had raises and promotions along the way.

Right now I'm assistant to the General Publicity Director—responsible for the production of 5,000,000 lines of advertising a year. I'M responsible for the training and improvement of a large corps of copywriters. I teach newcomers the ropes...and never a day passes which does not include instructions to these beginners. I interview applicants for jobs every day. I deal with over 100 executive buyers and their assistants...work with merchandise managers on promotions which include every kind of merchandise under the sun.

I'm in charge of a group of 26 captains selling War Savings Bonds and Stamps weekly to 561 employes of Famous-Barr Co. I've been President of the Store's Younger Executive Group...conducting meetings, securing speakers and planning the organization's activities for a year.

Somewhere in my attic is a diploma from Vanderbilt University signifying satisfactory completion of an A.B. course...and a couple of keys testifying to above-average grades. I've had experience on a couple of newspapers and have been engaged in Public Relations activities for Famous-Barr Co. for a number of years working with prominent members of St. Louis clubs, organizations and officials.

I have a working knowledge of problems of management and supply, merchandise, transportation, office management, personnel procurement and training.

I have taught Sunday School. I've written radio scripts. I can knock off a news release...fast! I can cook a steak that'll melt in your mouth or whip up a batch of spaghetti and mushrooms that'll knock your props out from under you with equal abandon.

Lest you lose yourself in the maze of my accomplishments, please put my ability as a Public Relations Counsel and as a Merchandise Man in the spotlight and if you have openings that call for a man with high qualifications in either field, I'm just the one you're looking for.

I'm 35, single, 1A in the draft, and while I feel I'll eventually reach the ranks of Officer Personnel after entering the Army through the ranks, I want to put my background to work where it will do the Army the most good.

You've broken up my happy home already. My roommate with whom I've lived for eight years is now in Miami in the Officers' Training School...and he has urged me to write you because he feels the work there will be a breeze for me. According to the information he sends, they are accepting men there now for training, some of them arriving two weeks after placing their applications. Please hurry...I've a bet with him that I'll come out of the Army with a higher rank than his...and he's off with a commission already and I'm still at the post.

Yours very truly,

E. T. S.
Assistant to
Publicity Director

ETS/gew

P. S.   I've had three years' training in the National Guard...was acting Sergeant at 18...Company L, 3rd Battalion, 117th Infantry, Tennessee National Guard, 1924-1927.

May 26, 1942.

Mr. E. T. S.
Assistant to Publicity Director,
Famous-Barr Company,
St. Louis, Missouri.

Dear Mr. S:

        This office is in receipt of your letter dated
May 22, 1942 in which you request appointment as a Second
Lieutenant in the Army of the United States. You will
find attached hereto the bar which you submitted with
your letter.

        It is suggested that you contact your nearest
recruiting office with a view to enlistment in the armed
forces. You are advised that in order to be eligible for
appointment to supply-procurement duties an applicant
must be classified as other than 1-A under Selective
Service and must have outstanding specialized qualifications.

        It is further suggested that you investigate
the possibility of applying for training in the Officer
Candidate Schools. This information can be obtained
from the nearest recruiting office.

                                    Very truly yours,

                                    W. D. SWANK,
                                    Captain, Air Corps,
Incl.   Asst. Adm. Executive.
    2nd Lt. Bar

---

(13) Catching a Swindler

One day in July 1941 I went to the barber shop to get a haircut. While waiting, I read an article in Friday *magazine about an international oil swindler. The two-page item included a picture of the man whose name was Allen A. Zoll. I recognized him as one who had applied at my office for a specialist reserve commission as an oil expert and executive. I had referred his application to our Supply Division to determine if they could use his services as an officer.*

At the time, he was about to be recommended for appointment. I immediately notified the Office of Special Investigations, the Federal Bureau of Investigation and Headquarters, Army Air Corps. As a result, he was apprehended and taken into custody.

(14) Summary of Official Travel

Departures from HQ, AC Materiel Division, Wright Field, Ohio

June 4, 1941	HQ, AAF, Washington, D.C.	Conference, OCAC
Jan. 1, 1942	HQ, AAF, Washington, D.C.	Personnel Problems
Jan. 20, 1942	HQ, AAF, Washington, D.C.	Manpower Report

Departures from HQ, AAF Materiel Command, Wright Field, Ohio

April 26, 1943	HQ, Mitchell Field, L.I. N.Y.	AF-wide Personnel Conference
July 25, 1943	HQ, AAF, Washington, D.C.	Personnel Conference
Aug. 15, 1943	HQ, AAF Midcentral Procurement District, Chicago, Ill.	New Assignment

Departures from HQ, AAF Midcentral Procurement District, Chicago, Ill.

Aug. 23, 1943	Indianapolis Area Office	Personnel Office and Allison Engine Plant
Sept. 16, 1943	Milwaukee Area Office	Staff Visit
Sept. 17, 1943	Milwaukee and Minneapolis Area Offices	Staff Visit
Sept. 18, 1943	Indianapolis, Ft. Wayne and Evansville Area Offices	Staff Visit
Sept. 21, 1943	South Bend Area Office	
Oct. 19, 1943	HQ, AAF Materiel Command	Command Personnel Conference
Nov. 2, 1943	HQ, AAF CAPD, Detroit, Mich.	Deferment Problems
Dec. 14, 1943	HQ, AAF Midwestern APD, Wichita, Kans.	Personnel Conference
Dec. 31, 1943	Milwaukee Area Office	Staff Visit
Jan. 6, 1944	Minneapolis Area Office and St. Paul Modification Center	Staff Visit
Jan. 10, 1944	HQ, AAF Materiel Command, Wright Field, Ohio	Personnel Problem
Jan. 13, 1944	Indianapolis Area Office	Personnel Problem
Jan. 22, 1944	HQ, AAF Central APD, Detroit, Mich.	War Bond Rally Deferment Policies
Feb. 1, 1944	Milwaukee Area Office	War Bond Rally Vocational School Visit
Feb. 8, 1944	Milwaukee Area Office Vocational School Visit	War Bond Rally
Feb. 18, 1944	HQ, AAF Materiel Command, Wright Field, Ohio	Personnel Policy
Feb. 22, 1944	Evansville Sub-Office	Toured Serval Aircraft Plants
March 2, 1944	Chicago and South Bend Area Offices and Studebaker Plant	Deferment Problems
March 3, 1944	Milwaukee Area Office	Deferment Problems
March 9, 1944	Chanute Field, Ill.	Recruitment
March 14, 1944	Chanute Field, Ill.	Recruitment
April 3, 1944	New York City	AAF Personnel Conference

April 27, 1944	Milwaukee Area Office	Deferment Problems
May 9, 1944	HQ, AAF Materiel Command, Wright Field, Ohio	Manpower Problems
May 23, 1944	Milwaukee Area Office	Talk to Inspection Trainees
June 14, 1944	South Bend Area Office	Inspection at Studebaker Plant
June 26, 1944	St. Louis, Mo.	AAF Materiel Command Personnel Conference
July 3, 1944	HQ, AMC, Wright Field, Ohio	Termination of Contracts Conference
July 25, 1944	South Bend Area Office	Deactivation of Area
Sept. 1, 1944	Milwaukee Area Office	RIF at Allis Chalmers Plant
Sept. 8, 1944	HQ, AFSC, Wright Field, Ohio	Transfer

Departures from HQ, ATSC, Wright Field, Ohio

Nov. 7, 1944	San Bernardino Air Depot, Calif.	ATSC Personnel Conference
Nov. 28, 1944	HQ, Pacific Overseas ATSC, Oakland, Calif.	New Assignment

Departures from HQ, POATSC, Oakland, Calif.

March 6, 1945	Los Angeles and Long Beach Intransit Depots	Inspection Trip
August 7, 1945	AAF Center, Orlando, Fla., AAF School	Personnel Mgt. Crse.
Oct. 2, 1945	Tacoma, Wash., Intransit Depot	Classification of Jobs
		Dade Bros. Contract
Feb. 16, 1946	HQ, ATSC, Wright-Patterson AFB, Ohio	Transfer

Departures from HQ, ATSC, Wright-Patterson AFB, Ohio

June 4, 1946	AAF Procurement Field Office, New York City	Personnel Problems

Approximately 35,000 miles

(15) Fighter Pilots Deserve More Than This!

**G. D. ZOOMIE
57th FIGHTER INTERCEPTOR GROUP PILOT
AFTER RETURNING TO THE Z.1.**

(16)

Was This <u>Really</u> the Prototype for WWII Fighter Aircraft?
TUT-ANKH-AMEN'S BATTLEPLANE

134

(17)

BT-9 Basic Trainers at Randolph Field, Texas, 1941.

Courtesy RFPL

(18)

Symbolic of America's engineering ingenuity and production skill is the Douglas XB-19A, largest airplane in the world, as it soars over Wright Field, Ohio, Headquarters of the Air Technical Service Command. New Allison engines give it a total of 10,400 horsepower—the equivalent of two modern steamlined trains.

Air Technical Service Command Photo

(19)

Major Stanley Umstead. Test Pilot XB-19A, largest airplane in the world.

(20)

WHAT PRICE AIR DEFENSE?

AMERICAN history has borne out one supreme point: The cost of freedom is quite high. In this supersonic age, let's look at it this way . . . The cost of enduring a few sonic booms in order to maintain our freedom is not nearly so high as the cost of losing the freedom to complain about Government operations, to vote for the political candidates of our choice (regardless of party affiliation), of attending whatever church we choose, of living where we please, of doing whatever work we like best, of travel within our country wherever we please at whatever time we choose, of the right to trial by jury of our peers, of protection against arbitrary arrest or seizure, of the right to bear arms to protect ourselves, of freedom of the press and of public meetings, and the many other freedoms that are guaranteed and protected by the country that your United States Air Force has the mission to defend.

(21)   **<u>Good for a Laugh</u>**

Mascot of an Air Force fighter squadron?!

BIBLIOGRAPHY

Center for Air Force History, USAF, Bolling AFB, D.C.

Lou Reda Publications, Inc., Easton, Pennsylvania

Personal Papers and Records

The Chicago Heights Star, Chicago Heights, Illinois, 1944

The Chicago Herald American, Chicago, Illinois, 1944

The Columbus Citizen, Columbus, Ohio, 1940

The Official Guide to the Army Air Forces, Washington, D.C., 1944

The Richmond Times Dispatch, Richmond, Virginia, 1990, 1993

INDEX